BIBLE VINDICATED.

A

SERIES OF ESSAYS

ON

AMERICAN SLAVERY.

WITH AN APPENDIX.

By ELDER JONAS HARTZEL,

PASTOR OF THE FIRST CHRISTIAN CHURCH, DAVENPORT, IOWA.

CINCINNATI:
PUBLISHED BY JOHN BOGGS.
1858.

PREFACE.

THE following Essays comprise a thorough examination of the whole subject of American Slavery, as far as the Bible is supposed to give it any countenance. That holy book is (we think) fully "vindicated" from the foul charge of being *pro-slavery.*

The Essays were originally written for the *North Western Christian Magazine*, but owing to their universal popularity among the friends of liberty and the Bible, and the strong solicitation of many of those who have read them, they are now presented in their present form. It has, with the assistance of the author, been carefully revised and corrected.

We commend the work to the favorable consideration of an enlightened public, believing it will be found an important auxiliary to the cause of humanity and religion. J. B.

CONTENTS.

INTRODUCTION.

I HAVE, for some time past, thought of reviewing the Bible on the subject of Slavery. Many brethren of intelligence dissenting, led me to suspect that there might be some error in my position. I have recently been called to the task; not, however, with a view to enlighten the Church on this subject, (a most humiliating necessity,) but to defend the Bible against the charge of being "pro-slavery in its tendency." This calumny was thrown upon the Book that contains the christian's faith and hope by an open-mouthed, long-tongued infidel, in the course of a series of lectures recently delivered in our place. When this missionary of infidelity referred to great names, great men, and great expounders of the Scriptures—preachers standing at the head of literary and theological institutions, etc., as concurring with him in this view of Bible teaching and tendency—the heart of the christian bled. Why? Because the christian could not say to the calumniator, you falsify, you have the concurrence of no such men. This feeling was the more pungent, from a conviction that the unbeliever was right; so far, at least, that the interpretation of the Bible, by such men, is the very bulwark of slavery, in so far as the church participates in the mischief. How painful to the christian, that this enemy of God's own Book, in which are contained all the elements of piety and morality, and hope for the future, has the concurrence of such renowned names, in what the Bible "admits and sustains;" differing *only* with them in the conclusions. They, indeed, affirming that as the Bible approves the "relation of master and slave for life,"—and as it is the christian's directory in all questions of right, therefore, we should acquiesce and offer no violence to the institution. But the unbeliever draws a widely different conclusion from the same premises, viz: that the Bible is not from God, but the production of wicked men, for God would not justify such a system of oppression as robs man of his humanity, and degrades him to the condition of a brute. Each, turning that in which they mutually agree to his own account, in his own way. The one to sustain slavery (American slavery, for we have no other) in the church and in the State, and the other to destroy confidence in the Bible, holding it up to public scorn and contempt, as being decidedly unjust and immoral in its tendency.

That slavery always has been demoralizing in its tendency will not be denied by its warmest adherents. If, then, the Bible, "both Moses and Paul sustain it," and the "tree is to be known by its fruit," we must ask pro-slavery christians to meet infidel abolitionists on the Bible controversy. A discussion between these parties could be readily agreed upon, as they now agree in the predicate. All that remains to be settled is simply, shall the Bible be employed to support American slavery, or shall the guarantee the Bible gives to slavery be employed for its own destruction?

We hold nothing in common with unbelievers in regard to the Bible. We have nothing to defend *but the book* on its own intrinsic merits. We are now engaged in answering the advocate of infidelity by a course of lectures, and shall give you the result of our review of the Bible upon the subject.

I am happy in the conviction that the Bible can be defended against pro-slavery christians and infidel abolitionists, many of which are making a great outcry against the evils of society, but are doing nothing towards correcting them, unless it is true, as these self-styled reformers affirm, that the minds of men must be emancipated from their reverence of the Bible before any thing can be affected in the way of reforming society: a position most false and self-destructive.

BIBLE VINDICATED.

ESSAY I.

I WILL now give the result of my review of what the Bible teaches on the subject of slavery. I was called upon by some of my fellow-citizens to answer the gross assaults of the infidel B. against the Bible. Among other charges of injustice and immorality was that of slaveholding, viz: that the Old and New Testaments justified the system of involuntary and perpetual slavery. Had we been slaveholders, or even entertained their sentiments, we should have regarded this portion of the infidel's sermons as a commendation to the Bible. We would have been edified. We would have taken no exceptions. No defense would have been called for, and no reply would have been made. Or, if the unbeliever had proven his position, we should have let the matter rest, as converts to slavery, or opponents to the Bible. But, as his argument consisted in unsustained assertions, and a few *nibbling criticisms*, we were of the same opinion still, that there was not a sanction for slavery—slavery proper, in the law of Moses.

To approach the subject in logical order, we inquire, first, how the Hebrews were to obtain their servants, and who were the specified subjects of servitude?

1st, then, "And if thy brother that dwelleth by thee be waxen poor, and be sold unto thee, thou shalt not compel him to serve as a bond-servant, but as a hired servant.

"But as an hired servant, and as a sojourner, he shall be with thee, and shall serve thee unto the year of jubilee:

"And then shall he depart from thee, both he and his children with him."—Lev. xxv: 39–42.

This looks more like paying debts than it looks like slavery. God taught the Jews to be honest. He gave them no bankrupt law, or exemption law. No legalized swindling was permitted under Moses. There is *no slavery in this statute,* but equity to the creditor and mercy to the debtor. By six years labor, not as a slave, but as a hired servant, he paid in all his indebtedness, and was taught a good lesson for the future.

When the six years' service had expired, the master was required to give his servant, at the time of his departure, an outfit. "And if thy brother, an Hebrew man, or an Hebrew woman, be sold unto thee, and serve thee six years, then in the seventh year thou shalt let him go free from thee. And when thou sendest him out free from thee, thou shalt not let him go away empty; Thou shalt furnish him liberally out of thy flock, and out of thy floor, and out of thy wine-press: of that wherewith the Lord thy God hath blessed thee thou shalt give unto him." To withhold was "sin." There is, then, no such thing as a Jew being a slave to a Jew in the law of Moses; but a law *to favor* the insolvent debtor. Infidelity has an "evil eye."

2d. If the bond-servants were not slaves, then there was no slavery under Moses, for the insolvent Jew, and the neighboring heathen, were the only *law*-specified servants. "Both thy bondmen and thy bondmaids, which thou shalt have, shall be of the heathen that are round about you; of them shall ye buy bondmen and bondmaids. Moreover, of the children of the strangers that do sojourn among you, of them shall ye buy, and of their families that are with you, which they begat in your land: and they shall be your possession. And ye shall take them as an inheritance for your children after you, to inherit them for a possession; they shall be your bondmen for ever: but over your brethren the children of Israel, ye shall not rule one over another with rigor."

If there was no other law limiting the time of servitude, this *would* be slavery.

It is a law-established *maxim*, that one section of law shall not be so "interpreted as to conflict with another." 1st, of the "heathen round about you," and of the "children of strangers that sojourn among you," and the "families they begat in your land: and they shall be your possession." 2d. They could not, according to the spirit of this law, purchase their bondmen in a promiscuous slave-market; from kidnappers, from "man-stealers," for then they could not know whether they were of the heathen round about them, or from a distant land. This is yet the more evident when the law says, "He that stealeth a man and selleth him, shall surely be put to death." Would this law have justified a Jew to purchase a stolen man? To purchase stolen goods is to encourage theft. To patronize theft and violence is to become accessory to the crime. The partaker is as bad as the thief, is a common sense adage. "Of the heathen round about you shall ye buy." The law required that they knew who they bought, and from whom they bought. This was an antidote against man-stealing and slave-markets. For now, the negotiation had to be between the purchaser and the individual bought, or such as had a better claim than a thief could establish. And if heathen husbands and fathers had no more affection for their wives and children than to sell them—there was no injustice in the law, as there was but one law in the religion of Moses, for the home-born and the stranger.—Ex. xii: 49. And but one civil code for the home-born and the stranger—Lev. xxiv: 22. 3d. "They shall be your bondmen for ever." The words "for ever" could not, at the farthest, extend farther than to the end of that dispensation. "The law and the prophets were until John," said the Messiah. The law was only a schoolmaster to the Jew until Christ. Then God said to three Jews, Peter, James, and John—Moses and Elias being present, "Hear my beloved Son." Their covenant was an "Everlasting Covenant." It was never changed, but it was abrogated. "Everlasting" and "For ever," when applied to things eternal in their being or duration, are equivalent with the word Eternal. But when applied to things of limited duration, they describe only the longest period of their existence. In Lev. x: 15, "for ever" means only the time of the law. "The heave shoulder," etc., to wave it for a wave offering before the Lord; and it shall be thine, and thy sons' with thee, by a statute for ever, as the Lord hath "commanded." A period less than fifteen hundred years. "But Hannah went not up; for she said unto her husband, *I will not go up* until the child be weaned, and then I will bring him, that he may appear before the Lord, and there abide for ever."—1 Sam. i: 22. Here "for ever" means the lifetime of a man. Other examples might be given. Bondmen "for ever" cannot extend beyond the longest period of Jewish servitude, which was forty-nine years. "And ye shall hallow the fiftieth year."—Lev. xxv: 10. "And ye shall return every man unto his family." Why distinguish the fiftieth year of release from any other? Not for the benefit of the Hebrew servants, for their release came every seven years.

The conspicuity given to the fiftieth year as a jubilee, must have contemplated other than Hebrew servants. "And ye shall hallow the fiftieth year, and proclaim liberty throughout all the land, to all the inhabitants thereof." This language is so explicit that no infidel can wrest it from its most obvious meaning. There was one class of servants released every seventh year, and two classes every fiftieth year. The Hebrew who did not accept his freedom on the seventh year, and the bond-servants. These were the "inhabitants of the land" for whose special benefit the jubilee was marked with so much importance. The release of the first class, being provided for, came at the end of every sixth, and would have come at the end of the forty-eighth year. The sounding of the "trumpet" in all the "land," and the "proclamation" of "liberty to all the inhabitants," has no meaning or significance, unless for the emancipation of those not released on the seventh year of their servitude.

3d. "And ye shall take them as an inheritance for

your children after you," etc. Their children could have no more in those bond-servants than was contained in the original title. If fifty years was the fixed time for a bond-servant, the heirs-in-law could hold them no longer, unless by some special enactment. Where is it? We call for it. Perpetual servitude enters into the very definition of slavery, the fortune of the offspring following the condition of the mother, from generation to generation. We say, then, with assurance, there was not a guarantee for slaveholding in the Mosaic law. It was a peculiar kind of servitude, differing in all its elements, from every slave code under heaven. The Hebrews were a peculiar people. Their religious and civil regulations were their own. And that system by which their domestic servitude was regulated, was unique, corresponding as a part with one great whole.

4th. It was affirmed that the law recognized servants as property. The evidence adduced was Ex. xxi. 20, 21, "And if a man smite his servant, or his maid, with a rod that he die under his hand, he shall be surely punished. Notwithstanding, if he continue a day or two, he shall not be punished; for he is his "money." Not literally his "money." Flesh and blood are not "money." By a familiar figure of speech, that for which money was paid is called "money." "Notwithstanding, if he continue a day or two, he shall not be punished, for he is his money." This part of the law was to bear upon the motive of the master; showing that he did not intend to inflict a fatal blow upon his servant. The master wanted his service—had paid his "money" for him. Therefore he did not intend to kill him. Men do not wantonly throw away their money in this way. "He is his money." The purchaser wanted a *living*, not a dead servant. "If he continue a day or two, it, the law, may presume that the smiting was not the cause of the servant's death, or, if it was, the master ought not to be punished, for his object was not to destroy his servant—he was not influenced by a malignant motive, and therefore, to be regarded as an accident, rather than a criminal act.

This, I believe, is the only passage relied upon to prove that the law acknowledged property in man. The property feature is the most important element in any system of slavery, ancient or modern, hence, the fullness, and definiteness, of the legislation in all slave codes on that head. If the divine law was the same in this respect, why so obscure on this point. Only one passage, and that an incidental one, favoring the interpretation above, rather than the property relation. Why no law regulating sales, and the recovering of fugitives? If the law of Moses made servants chattels, it is a piece of blind legislation in this particular, wholly unlike itself in all other enactments. But as our opponents have all so signally failed, in proving their affirmation, we shall proceed to establish a negative, and respectfully submit, that the servants in the Old Testament were *not* property.

1st. Servants are not so classified, "Thou shalt not see thy brother's ox, or his sheep go astray, and hide thyself from them: thou shalt in any case bring them again unto thy brother.—And if thy brother be not nigh unto thee, or if thou know him not, then shalt thou bring it unto thine own house, and it shall be with thee until thy brother seek after it, and thou restore it to him again. In like manner shalt thou do with his ass; and so shalt thou do with his raiment; and with all lost things of thy brother's, which he has lost, and thou hast found, shalt thou do likewise; thou mayest not hide thyself." Here we have a list of property. Property liable to go astray, and to be lost. The straying "ox," "sheep," or "ass," was to be "returned to his owner," and so of the "lost garment, or any lost thing." If the owner was not known, the finder was required to "take care of it until the owner would call for it, when it should be delivered." Servants are at least as much inclined to run away from their masters as "oxen," "sheep," or "asses," are to stray from their owners. If then, the Hebrew masters held their servants as property, and the owners of this kind of property were liable to the same losses, why not place human property in the category to which it belongs? The omission, if it be an omission, is unaccountable. The law enforced the most rigid justice between man and man, therefore, that which the law recognized as property, was in all cases to be returned to the rightful owner. The fugitive "ox" and "ass" were to be arrested, and driven back to the owner, but the fugitive servant was not to be returned to his master. "Thou shalt not deliver unto his master the servant which is escaped from his master unto thee. He shall dwell with thee, even among you, in that place which he shall choose in one of thy gates, where it liketh him best: thou shalt not oppress him." If the servant was the property of his master, the law of Moses made him so. And here the same law says this item of property shall not be delivered to the owner. Is Moses against Moses? Did he give the master ownership in the person of his servant in one section of the law, and in another section, say he shall not have his own? Will we charge such crooked legislation upon the lawgiver of Israel? "Thou shalt not deliver unto his master," &c., was controverting the legality of the master's claim to the person and the labor of his servants. To affirm that this law had respect to servants, escaping from *heathen masters only*, will not help the infidel. For, then, we ask for the proof. Does the law say heathen masters? No! Is there any thing in the statute from which such a limitation can be inferred? No! not unless in the phrase "*even* among you:" "even" is a supplied word. To allow such an inference, is to make the Bible what sceptics say it is, an "instrument that may be set to play any tune you please."

Why should the law allow to a Jew property in his servant, and not to a Gentile? One of two positions must be assumed. 1st. Master, in the text, applies to all masters; or, 2nd. That Gentiles could not be masters—could not own man as property, not having a divine warrant, or permit, from God, to be *slave owners*. If the infidel will take the first, then the law did not recognize the servants held by the Jews, as property; if the latter then the Old Testament is not chargeable with any form of Gentile slavery. Inasmuch as God never commanded a Gentile in the Law, the Prophets, or the Psalms, to enslave man, woman, or child. The first acquits the law from the property feature—then no slavery. In either case, the law of Moses is not the patron of human slavery, and the charge is false.

We have now examined the law, and find nothing like slavery in it. Next in order will be the Prophets, where we shall find slavery, the "Yoke," but without command of God, or the sanction of the Prophets. There we shall find the *type* of our own times—with more than a sprinkling of abolitionism.

ESSAY II.

In the prophetic writings we find slavery—slavery proper. The Jews were not pleased with their law of servitude. The jubilee! yes! the jubilee! what a trouble. The years of release came round so quickly, when every Hebrew servant, by the law of his God, was at once free from indebtedness and from his master. What a trouble now! who shall do the work? Must we, our sons and our daughters? We are unaccustomed to labor. Meanwhile we must do the best we can, and supply the place of these freed ones as soon as possible. But there was yet another trouble about these times; when the servant was free, the master was *not* free, but was debtor to the freed servant. "And when thou sendest him out free from thee, thou shalt not let him go away empty. Thou shalt furnish him liberally out of thy flock, and out of thy floor, and out of thy winepress, of that wherewith the Lord thy God hath blessed thee, thou shalt give unto him." Deut. xv: 13, 14. The year of the "release" was the cause of all this trouble. And as in other cases, when justice and equity are demanded at the hand of the unrighteous, they will rebel. "At the end of seven years, let ye go every man his brother a Hebrew which hath been sold unto thee; and when he hath served thee six years, thou shalt let him go free from thee; but your fathers hearkened not unto me, neither inclined their ear. And ye were now turned and had done right in my sight in proclaiming liberty, every man to his neighbor; and ye had made a covenant before me in the house which is called by my name: But ye turned and polluted my name, and caused every man his servant, and every man his handmaid whom he had set at liberty at their pleasure to return, and brought them into subjection, to be unto you for servants and for handmaids," Jer. xxxiv: 14, 15, 16. This was slavery *outriyht.* The year of release came—it passed—but they held on to their slaves. Their fathers had done so before them. The Jews abused their liberty, their legal privileges, and from *servant*-holders they became *slave*-holders, and slave-*catchers.* They rebelled against the law of the Lord, and were a law unto themselves. If they treated their own poor brethren in this way, is it probable that they would treat the heathen bond-servant better? If they disregarded the law in the one case, they surely would in the other. If their cupidity would contravene a law favorable to their own brethren, they could, without any *qualms* of conscience, desecrate the *fiftieth* year jubilee, and sink their pro-slavery fangs yet deeper into the bosom of the heathen bondman. Such was the state of affairs in the days of Jeremiah, and had been long before his time.

But the reader will ask, how came they at this time to let their servants go free? If he will read the xxxiv chapter of Jeremiah from the eighth verse, he will find it was the result of an *anti-slavery convention,* as reported by that prophet. Zedekiah called this meeting. It was held in the temple. "The princes of Judah and the princes of Jerusalem, the eunuchs, and the priests, and all the people of the land," were in attendance. This was a *national* convention. They entered into solemn covenant before the Lord, that they would let their servants go free. To ratify this covenant, and make the obligation binding, they " cut the calf in twain and passed between the parts thereof." Every thing was calculated to make the occasion solemn and impressive. The convention was called by royal authority. " This is the word that came unto Jeremiah from the Lord, after that the king Zedekiah had made a covenant with all the people, which were at Jerusalem, to proclaim liberty unto them." The king required a pledge from the people, that they would liberate their servants now by them degraded to the condition of slaves. They made the promise, and with the most solemn formalities ratified this covenant, and the sincerity of their intentions. The present condition of the nation would wake them up to a sense of their guilt.

Eight years before this the king of Babylon had besieged Jerusalem, " And took the king of Judah and with him ten thousand captives, including the princes, the men of valor, the best of the crafts-men, and all that were strong and apt for war:" 2 Kings, ch. 24. This was an interesting anti-slavery meeting. It was an exciting time. It was a popular movement. Zedekiah was the prime mover. The "princes" and "priests," with the "people," went for immediate emancipation. "Then they obeyed and let them go;" verse 10. "But afterwards they turned and caused the servants and the handmaids whom they had let go free to return, and brought them unto subjection;" verse 11.

"And ye were now turned and had done right in my sight, in proclaiming liberty every man to his neighbor." "But ye turned and polluted my name, and caused every man his servant to return and brought them into subjection." "Therefore thus saith the Lord, ye have not hearkened unto me in proclaiming liberty, every one to his brother, and every man to his neighbor; behold I proclaim a liberty for you saith the Lord, to the sword, to the pestilence, and to the famine." "And Zedekiah king of Judah, and his princes, will I give into the hands of their enemies." "Behold I will command, saith the Lord, and cause them (the Chaldeans) to return to this city, and they shall fight against it and take it," etc. In less than three years this prophetic *threat was executed.* The king and whole posse of slaveholders, were slaves to Nebuchadnezzar, king of Babylon. He "returned" with his army in the ninth year of Zedekiah, besieged the city two years, until the "famine prevailed in the city and there was no bread for the people in the land." The city was broken up. The king and all the men of war fled by night. The victors "pursued," overtook the fugitive army and king on the plains of Jericho, "slew the sons of Zedekiah before his eyes," and then they "put out his eyes," and the captain of the guard carried all the people "away," save the "poor of the land." God liberated the slaves, and let the masters enjoy the sweets of slavery. "Behold I proclaim a liberty for you, saith the Lord!" How descriptive and how just this *irony!* What a precious liberty these slave-masters enjoyed in Babylon!

My thoughts now turn upon the unfortunate Zedekiah. Why visit him with such unmeasured severity?

Did he not convoke this great convention for the abolition of slavery in his kingdom? Did he not make a covenant with his people that they would liberate their slaves? Did he not require from them the usual confirmation to covenant engagements? Yes; he did all this. What more could he do? He was surely a good abolitionist in sentiment. He also spoke out against the evil, and took measures to suppress it. Ah! poor man! He *failed* in the important point. He did not *enforce* obedience to the covenant. This he had a right to do. Nay, it was his duty as the executive of the nation to enforce obedience to the law, and see that every Hebrew servant and all bond servants were set at liberty when their time of servitude had expired. He knew his subjects were living in open violation of the law of the Lord. He saw the need of reform, but was wanting in firmness to bring it about. Therefore, instead of saying to masters this is the year of release; now let your servants go free and furnish them liberally out of your flock and floor," etc., he adopted a *compromising* policy, and made a covenant with them, that they would obey God. And when they violated this covenant he winked at their iniquity, and suffered the servants to be recalled into perpetual and unconditional slavery.

To take sides with the *poor* against the *rich*, what a hazardous business! What havoc with popularity! Zedekiah was the *prototype* of many in our own times. They see the wrongfulness of slavery; they confess it; they will sometimes speak a hard word against it; and if by some popular movement slavery could be abolished, they would give their vote. "They are as much opposed to slavery as anybody, but;" yes!

But, we must be careful *when* we talk about it, and *where* and before *whom*. The pulpit is not the right place, and in some college halls it is wholly inadmissible, if slaveholders should be in attendance. Not to observe these rules, is to be reckless on the subject of good morals. This, however, may also involve the question of time and place. The time was, and not long since, even in Ohio, when to advocate anti-slavery sentiments was considered so grossly immoral, that the preacher usually received his stipends in tar, feathers, and rotten eggs, when they could be had. But now the preacher is paid with a better and more desirable currency, for the advocacy of the same sentiments.

Morality and right on some questions are as variable as public sentiment. What may be regarded as strictly moral, north of a certain line, may not be so esteemed south of it. But time may even effect a change south as it has north, inasmuch as morality and righteousness on the subject are not *immutable.* The slave trade was both good and right until the last night of December, 1808; but on the morning of the first day of January, 1809, the same trade was piracy, man-stealing, a crime punished with death. There is as yet no settled standard of morality on this subject, outside of the Bible. The morality of that old book on the subject of slavery, is not current in some latitudes. But as long as it contains this solemn charge, "Cry aloud, spare not, lift up thy voice like a trumpet and show my people their transgressions, and the house of David their sins." "Is not this the fast (abstinence) that I have chosen? to loose the bands of wickedness, to undo the heavy burdens, and to let the oppresed go free, and that ye break every yoke?"

it can not in the sight of God be immoral to do what he has commanded.

But to return to the Jews. The clear and well defined law of Moses, with all its weighty sanctions, could not secure to servants their freedom at the appointed time. The nation conquered by a foreign despot, and the better part of the people in positive slavery in a distant heathen city; the will of their king, and their own convictions of duty and right, consummated and ratified in solemn covenant; their better sentiments getting the ascendancy over avarice; all could not break their hold upon their slaves. Conviction relaxed the iron sinew for a short time. The Lord said, "Ye had turned and had done right," but they soon repented for having "done right," and pursued the emancipated, the glad-hearted, and by violence brought them again into bondage. Neither gold nor silver, nor any thing under heaven, is held with a firmer grasp than the poor slave. The pleadings of suffering humanity, the interests of humanity, the honor of humanity, the good of the State, the honor and interests of religion, the credit of the Bible, and the voice of God in it, are all unavailing. The master will hold on to his property in human flesh. So valuable that a living writer once said, "None but God can own a man," but men aspire to be gods in more ways than one. For men to invade the divine prerogative, is not a new thing under the sun. To own God's image impressed upon humanity by himself, and to degrade that image to a chattel, is not regarded as any stretch of authority by many professed christians.

So the Jews reasoned, and so they did; but God vindicated his own prerogative to ownership in man.

For as soon as they departed from the law of servitude he had given them, and they became slave-owners, he required for their slaves an immediate emancipation. "Ye have not hearkened unto me, in proclaiming liberty." "Behold I proclaim unto you a liberty!" But we must also hear Isaiah and Nehemiah on this subject.

ESSAY III.

WE will now hear Isaiah and Nehemiah, as intimated in our last. "Is not this the fast that I have chosen? To loose the bands of wickedness, to undo the heavy burdens and let the oppressed go free, and that ye break every yoke." "Then shall thy light break forth as the morning, and thy health shall spring forth speedily: and thy righteousness shall go before thee, the glory of the Lord shall be thy rereward. Then shalt thou call, and the Lord will answer; thou shalt cry, and he shall say, Here am I. If thou take away from the midst of thee, the yoke, the putting forth of the finger and speaking vanity."—Isaiah lviii: 6, 8, 9.

Between Jewish servitude, according to the law of Moses, and Jewish slavery, as reported by the Prophets, there is an irreconcilable difference. God allowed the former, but disallowed the latter. In their early history they had servants, but in their subsequent history they had slaves.

In the first period, say from Moses to Isaiah, there is no language in their records descriptive of slavery, and therefore no anti-slavery pleadings.

Can words be more descriptive of absolute slavery, than the above extract? "Let the oppressed go free!" This "oppression" was not simply an "oppression" of the helpless or the poor. The command is not to cease to oppress such, but to "*let the oppressed go free.*" Many of the oppressed are "free," were always "free," can leave their masters when they please, and when to their interest do so. The fast God had chosen consisted—

1st. In "loosing the bands of wickedness;"

2d. "Undoing heavy burdens;"

3d. "Letting the oppressed go free," and to "break every yoke."

Here are three specific forms of wickedness to be abstained from, and how was this to be done? In the things commanded, we have the imperative words and the descriptive words. "Loose" in the first is imperative, "bands of wickedness" is descriptive. In the second, "undo" is imperative, "heavy burdens" descriptive. In the third, the words "oppressed" is the descriptive, and "let" "go free" the imperative. To do justice to the poor and dependent, God required the Jews to "undo" the "heavy burdens," but for another class of sufferers he required immediate emancipation. Pecuniary embarrassment of some kind subjected the one to the "heavy burdens" and an unlawful relation, the other to oppression, *therefore* the God of the oppressed does not say to the oppressor, "correct the abuses of this institution," leave off your oppression, "treat your slaves right," but "let" the "oppressed," by you deprived of freedom, "go free," "and that ye break every yoke." "If thou take away from the midst of thee the yoke, the putting forth of the finger"—a sign of contempt. "Ah! you are a slave, you are of mean, low birth, *you are a nigger, fit only to be my slave*," etc.

"The putting forth of the finger and speaking vanity," are concomitants of slavery. Before one man can enslave another, he must have contemptible views both of his person and his personal rights. These views are of easy subdivision between the slaveholder and his family, and lordly neighbors. They become more and more confirmed by possession, until the "finger" of scorn, and the most emphatic language of reproach are, as matters of course, of every-day occurrence. The respectful bow and address are not more necessarily associated with other relations than the "finger" of scorn and words of insult are with this. That God whose spirit directed the pen of the prophet Isaiah, prompted the utterance "let the oppressed go free, break every yoke." "If thou take away from thy midst the yoke, the putting forth of the finger and speaking vanity;" "then shall thy light break forth as the morning;" "then shalt thou call and the Lord will answer it."

It is unmistakably certain, that the Jews in the days of Isaiah had become slaveholders. For, had they observed their law of servitude, they would not have been charged with "oppression," neither would that servitude have been represented under the strong figure of "a yoke," which God required them to "break," and let those whom they had compelled to bear that yoke "go free." The jubilees would have freed their servants at the appointed time, hence there would have been no occasion for Isaiah's abolitionism. "Let the oppressed go free, and break every yoke."

"When you shall keep the fast the Lord has chosen, then shall your light break forth as the morning," etc. They would not "break the yoke," they did not "put away the finger" of contempt, or, to drop the figure, they would not manumit their slaves as God commanded them, and their darkness became still darker, and their chastisements more severe. One hundred years after this faithful pleading to put away the yoke (slavery) from their "midst," their king and ten thousand of the best of their people, were carried down to Babylon, to the greatest slave market in the world. Soon after this calamity, Zedekiah made a covenant with the nation to let their slaves "go free." They did so, but afterwards brought them back again into bondage. Now the word of the Lord came to Jeremiah—"Therefore, thus saith the Lord: you have not hearkened unto me in proclaiming liberty," etc.; "behold I proclaim a liberty for you, saith the Lord, to the sword, the pestilence, and the famine," etc. In three years from this time, this promised liberty was sent to them by the Chaldean army, and all, save a few of the meanest of the nation (perhaps the slaves,) were slaves to the king of Babylon. One would suppose, indeed, that the command of God by Isaiah would have been obeyed, or that they would have heeded the last admonition by Jeremiah, and have liberated their slaves. But no, seventy years of the most rigorous slavery in Babylon failed to cure them of their love for slavery. No sooner was the nation emancipated and permitted to enjoy freedom in their own land, than the aristocrats began again their traffic in human flesh. "Then I consulted with myself, and I rebuked the nobles and the rulers, and said unto them, ye exact usury, every one from his brother. And I set a great assembly against them, and I said unto them, we after our ability have redeemed our brethren the Jews, which were sold to the heathen, and will you even sell your brethren? Or shall they be sold unto us? Then they held their peace and found nothing to answer. Also, I said, it is not good that ye do: ought ye not to walk in the fear of our God, because of the reproach of the heathen our enemies?" Neh. v: 7, 8, 9. A scandal to Judaism. *Reader, understand.*

The advocacy of anti-slavery sentiments by the prophets had some effect upon the nation; and their experience in Babylon perhaps more. In the time of Nehemiah the great reformer, the slaveocracy were a minority; the mass of the nation were anti-slavery. The nobility and the rulers were the only advocates in the nation. But fortunately the reformer of the nation was a thorough-going abolitionist. He roused up the indignation of a great assembly against the few slaveholders. He cared not for their noble blood or their official standing. He put them to shame before all their people. We, said he, have done all we could to redeem our brethren from slavery, and you are "selling them and causing them to be sold unto us." You are not walking in the fear of our God. You are giving the heathen, our enemies, an occasion to reproach us and our religion. Condemned and conscience-smitten, they "held their piece and found nothing to answer."

I have now abbreviated into a synopsis my review and defense of the Old Testament, in this and the preceding articles; and shall say, with kindly feeling, that the man who will charge the Old Testament with being the *patron* of slavery, does so ignorantly or wickedly. And now I will say, what I did not then say, viz: the man who will appeal to this book in defense of slavery, to justify any system of slavery, does so ignorantly or wickedly.

RECAPITULATION.

1st. The law of Moses allowed the Jews to have servants.

2d. It fixed the time of servitude at six years, and forty-nine years.

3d. The law did not classify servants as property, but as inhabitants of the land.

4th. Every species of property, lost or strayed from its owner, was by the law to be returned, but the fugitive servant was not to be returned.

5th. So long as the Jews regulated their domestic servitude according to the law, it is not called "yoke."

6th. In the time of Isaiah, the Jews had *metamorphosed* their system of servitude into a system of absolute slavery; then God called it a "yoke," and commanded them to break it immediately, and "let the oppressed go free."

7th. In the days of Jeremiah they did let their Hebrew slaves "go free."

8th. God said, "Ye had now done right."

9th. Afterwards they repented for having done right, and pursued their slaves and brought them back into servitude; then God pronounced upon them the heaviest judgment that befel the nation, until its final catastrophe for the offense.

10th. After the nation returned from seventy years

slavery to their own land and the enjoyment of free dom, the "nobles" and "rulers" of the nation became slaveholders again.

11th. Nehemiah the reformer, "rebuked" the "no bles" and the "rulers" for this offense, and the re proach they had brought upon the nation.

12th. He "put a great assembly against" these offenders. *In modern parlance, an indignation meeting.*

Finally. Happy that reformer, who, like Nehemiah, will take sides with God against the oppressor!

A reformation with slavery, the pointing of the "finger" and speaking "vanity" in its "midst!" What think you brethren? Is this the reformation God has "chosen?" Did you not begin reformation in *anti-slavery?* and will you now make reformation perfect in *pro-slavery?* Shall minor evils be corrected or repudiated, and this "maximum of all evils" remain as before? Brethren, will you be *dumb*, or will you *speak?* *Speak* in a way to be heard. If your voice will not obtain freedom for the oppressed, it may do something toward removing the "reproach" of our enemies. God will hold you responsible for what you can do.

ESSAY IV.

In our last we took our leave of Moses and the Prophets, of Hebrew servitude as approved and regulated by the law of Moses, and Jewish slavery as reproved and condemned by the Prophets, and abolished by the judgments of God sent upon a nation of oppressors.

We now open to another department, and shall hear what other parties have to offer by way of *divine sanctions* in this great contest.

And by way of settling some preliminaries, we shall say,

1. That Jesus Christ and his Apostles had to take the world as it was, as *they* found it, its religious and civil institutions as they were, and make the best of the world that infinite wisdom and benevolence could on moral principles.

2. To destroy sin, and to save the sinner, are leading elements in God's moral government, at least so far as this world is concerned. These principles pervade every dispensation of God's will to man, from the first to the second Adam. God has changed his forms and appliances, but his principles never. These are immutable. So far as this has been effected have the ends of the divine administration been accomplished.

The divine clemency looks upon the sinner first as the child of misfortune. This favorable view has opened to man a door of mercy. But if the sinner will not enter, then he stands before God in the light of a culprit.

The compassionate Redeemer read his own commission in the Synagogue at Nazareth. "And when he had opened the book he found the place where it was written, The spirit of the Lord is upon me, because he has anointed me to preach the Gospel to the poor! He hath sent me to heal the broken-hearted, to preach deliverance to the captive, and recovering of sight to the blind, to set at liberty them that are bruised. To preach the acceptable year of the Lord."

With these instructions God sent his Son on a mission to this world. Look at the specifications in this commission. The words "poor," "broken-hearted," "captives," "blind," "bruised," describe the condition of those for whose benefit this mission was instituted. "To preach the acceptable year of the Lord." To make compensation to the unfortunate *therefore* am I come, to remove the cause, and save from poverty, broken-heartedness, captivity, etc.

Such then is the caption to the Gospel—the heading to the work of Jesus Christ. So far as the then existing institutions and relations tended to bring man into, and hold him in the condition here described, these were to be corrected. He would make another effort by new appliances to destroy sin, and save the poor unfortunate sinner. For in some important aspect his present sorrows are not of his own choosing, or his own mismanagement.

With this preface we will approach some of the out-posts. The civil government was an absolute pagan despotism. Jesus Christ and his Apostles were tax-payers but not voters. They could not propitiate the government to favor the "broken-hearted," and the "bruised." The civilization was of pagan type. The bible had nothing to do directly in modeling society out of Judea. Christianity was not then responsible for the order of society, as it now is in what are called christian lands. Whatever was incompatible with sound christian morality had to be corrected. This they aimed to do and did do, by converting the world to christianity. Converting was their *fulcrum*, and to teach and perfect the converted was their only *lever* to raise up the sunken mass. Not to convert would have been *failure*. Not to make the converted better in their circumstances and relations, purer, holier, happier in their persons, would have been *defeat*, and the "acceptable year of the Lord" would have been but a golden dream, as many of the so-called reformations have been.

"Go, preach the Gospel to every creature," is the most philanthropic, the boldest, the grandest oracle ever heard by mortal man, and contains more of the aggressive than the literature of the world beside. Under this broad behest, the Apostles go forth to convert the nations to righteousness. They must not pass one "creature." They must make a tender of the Gospel to the Jew, to the Gentile, to the white man, to the black man, to the master, to the slave, to the polygamist, and to his wives. But right *here* we turn up a difficulty. Jesus Christ gave no countenance to a plurality of wives, shall they withhold the Gospel? No, "preach it to every creature." Shall they require the polygamist to repudiate all his wives save one? The law of God will allow him one, which of the three or more may he retain? They are all equally his wives, he is under the same obligations to all. To make separation a condition of acceptance, would have been unjust. The Gospel can not be the minister of unrighteousness. Let them come in. He took these several women when no law forbade him, but law justified him. It was not sin to him then, "for by the law is the knowledge of sin," but let it spread no further. It did spread no further. The Apostles' teachings put a check to it. Would any preacher of the Gospel now do as the Apostles did? Under the same circumstances, they should follow their example. But where christian morality and christian civilization have preceded conversion, we require a formal separation. In the latter case we would be governed by the Apostles' teachings, and say that every man is to have "his own *wife* and every woman her own *husband*."

If the Apostles had justified polygamy it would have continued in the Church as before. But having been abolished by christian civilization, its former extenuation is for ever removed in all christian lands. The simple fact that Apostles baptized polygamists in their day and order of society is no evidence that we should do so now. Not one of my brethren in the ministry would do so, no, not *even* those who baptize slaveholders would baptize a polygamist now. They would say, and with great propriety, the teachings of Jesus Christ and of his Apostles, are opposed to this relation, and the man that has more than one wife now has nothing to palliate his case. With Jesus Christ and the Apostles before me, I will venture the affirmation that no converted man could become a polygamist. The conclusion then is, that to save the sinner the Apostles took the parties in polygamy into the Church, but left the sinful custom outside. This was both mercy and justice, under the then existing circumstances, granting some extenuation on account of former ignorance. As christianity progressed the ignorance of past ages was dispelled, and the evils of society were rebuked in advance of conversion. This being done on a scale so broad, the proclamation of the Gospel was emphatically "The acceptable year of the Lord" to the "poor," the "broken-hearted," the "captives," etc. With the consent of the christian world I may say the Gospel is *anti*-polygamy. To take the opposite position would be too monstrous.

To correct the sins of society—we mean organic sins—as, when the head and heart of the nation are fixed upon a specific evil—that evil must by some means be taken into hand, otherwise it is unmanageable. To bring such national *lustings* under corrective treatment, a degree of allowance must sometimes be granted, and lesser evils must become matters of *temporary sufferance*, in order to prevent, or correct *graver ones*. The infinitely wise and benevolent God has ever acted upon this principle. When the nation of Israel rejected God as their King, and *lusted* for another, that they might be in fashion with their neighbors, he yielded to their repeated importunities and gave them one, not because the demand of the nation for a king was right, or pleasing to himself, but as a choice between evils. For when he told the people by the mouth of Samuel, that their king would afflict them sorely, they believed him not, but said, "give us a king," etc.

Now, hear a comment upon this instructive fact: "O, Israel, thou hast destroyed thyself, but in me is thy help. I will be thy king; where is any *other* that can save thee in all thy cities and thy judges, of whom thou saidst, give us a king and princes? I gave thee a king in mine *anger*, and took him away in my *wrath*." Hosea xiii: 9, 10, 11. So deep-rooted was this unholy desire, that it had to be granted, or the nation destroyed. "And Saul was anointed king over Israel." God gave the Jews a king, *therefore* the desire to have a king, was well-pleasing in his sight.

The Apostles admitted polygamists to enter the Church, *therefore* polygamy is right, *say the inhabitants of Utah.* God allowed slaveholders to enter the Church, *therefore* slavery is right, for God has given it his sanction, *so says* the slaveholder and his *apologist.* God gave the Jews a king, now let us reject King Jesus, and have another to rule over us, would be the same in *fact* and in *logic.* But God also recognized the relation of kings and subjects in Israel, and made their reciprocal duties the subject of special legislation—*did he approve the relation?* Is this conclusion legitimate? Let the prophet Hosea decide. "I gave thee a king in mine anger, and took him away in my wrath." To elaborate this principle in the divine government a little farther, we will hear from David: "They soon forgot his works, they waited not for his counsel, but lusted exceedingly and tempted God in the desert. And he gave them their request, but sent leanness in their soul. Psalm cvi: 13, 14, 15. Again, "Moses, because of the hardness of your hearts, suffered you to put away your wives; but from the beginning it was not so." Matt. xix: 8. In this way God kept the Jews in abeyance. In mercy, he permitted in given cases, what was not in harmony with strict moral principle. That through his forbearance he might save the nation from total apostacy, and retain in the world the knowledge of his name.

But hence to argue, that because "God gave the Jews a king," gave the things they "lusted after in the desert," and "suffered them to put away their wives," that, therefore, God justified them in these things, is to argue most fallaciously. Such conclusions are dishonorable to God and the Bible, and positively, "*turning the grace of God into lasciviousness.*" The polygamy and slavery of the New Testament belong to this category. When the gospel was promulgated, society was so entangled with these relations, that the masses of the poor, were either *degraded wives or degraded slaves.* To have insisted upon divorcement and manumission, as conditions of salvation, would have been virtually an abandonment of the regeneration of the world by the gospel. The rich, the influential, were in favor of these institutions; the weak were under their power. The popular ear could never have been reached by the Apostles, if they had assailed directly these time-honored, law-established usages. It is indeed questionable whether the christian religion could have been established at all. In that event these evils would have continued until the end of time to afflict and curse mankind. To remove the evils, they must be "*taken in hand.*" To make them manageable, they must be brought under the jurisdiction of christianity. To accomplish this, the gospel had to be made available to those who were involved in these relations. Therefore, the invitation, "Come, all ye that labor and are heavy laden," was to all classes.

There is a striking analogy between polygamy and slavery; both are of human creation. The first originated in the lust of the flesh, the second in the lust of forbidden gain. The former being condemned by the law of the land, and the latter legalized, affects not the quality of the institutions, nor yet their coincidence. Neither can any man on earth give a valid reason why there should be legal guarantees for slavery, and none for polygamy. Is not the lust of "*sordid gain*" as mischievous in its various workings, as hateful to heaven, and ruinous to man, as sternly condemned by the word of God, as is the lust of the flesh? And the conclusion is both safe and charitable, that the man who is a slaveholder because the "law of the State permits him to be such," would also be a polygamist, if the law of the State did not forbid him.

Slaveholding in the days of the Apostles was a thing of "good report." Men became slaveholders without *rebuke*. In these United States it was always of "bad report," of most doubtful morality. The majority of both Church and State have so regarded the Institution from the infancy of our country. The man that becomes a slaveholder now, does so in despite of this fact. The light has shone upon this dark and doubtful concern.

The Roman slaveholder had not the light in advance; the American slaveholder has the light, and "loves the darkness." The circumstances of slaveholders before the christian era, and since that period are dissimilar; as dissimilar as pagan and christian civilization. Therefore, christian ministers refuse Church membership to polygamists. Why not refuse the same to slaveholders?

So much by way of preliminary. In our next we shall examine the New Testament, and give the result of our former review.

ESSAY V.

We have now opened the New Testament, and shall ask the reader to read again Essay IV. of this series. For, that system of Slavery with which the Apostles and first christians had to do, differed widely in many essential aspects from that which so grievously afflicts the American people, both Church and State.

That was not negro slavery, ours is. The right then to hold slaves was not based upon national inferiority or color, as is ours, but the right of conquest, claiming the persons of the conquered upon the same ground they did their lands and chattels. This was understood when the belligerent nations met each other upon the field of battle. The alternatives between which hostile nations had to choose, were, to surrender their national independence, with the liability of becoming slaves, or to maintain it by an appeal to the sword.

Hence, the captives offered in the slave market were often whiter than the bidders, and more learned than their masters. Clerks, amanuenses, philosophers, and orators, commanded the highest price. "*And the price, from ten to seventy pieces of gold, was determined by their age, their strength, and their education.*" Gib. Rome: vol. 4, page 279.

There was some thing at least apparently even-handed and magnanimous in their way of obtaining slaves. They could make as fair a show of right to their slaves as we can to the conquered Territory of Mexico. But what show of right can America make to her four millions of slaves? This question leads out something the most *contemptible and mean that ever blackened* the history of any nation since the world began. German, Spanish, English, and American avarice is the origin of American Slavery, and not manly conquest. Cupidity, the most sordid—a cold-hearted selfishness, with which only the most malignant of fallen spirits could inspire the most corrupt heart of fallen humanity, is the origin of our system of Slavery. Away yonder in Africa is a colored race—a weak and ignorant people. This despised, defenceless race might easily be captured or decoyed and shipped to other ports and sold for slaves. In this conception we have the origin of American Slavery. When this lust was conceived it brought forth sin—slavers—crews of pirates (manstealers) bound for the shores of Africa—with manacles for the hands, and chains for the feet—*all aboard*, sailed for English ports well freighted with the spoils of theft and robbery. Now markets are opened—auctioneers are obtained—bidders are invited—sales go off briskly—the new kind of chattel becomes the subject of English legislation—Slavery spreads rapidly through the kingdom—is extended to all her islands adapted to slave labor—sent with the colonists to America—and, finally, Slavery becomes a subject of American legislation; and every State in this great confederacy can have slaves if it will so decide—and traffic in the bodies and souls of men to its heart's desire.

A pebble may turn the current of a river; a thought may revolutionize an empire; and the conception to acquire wealth by stealing men and women has agitated kingdoms—will yet shake America like a reed, and has, and yet is making millions *mourn*.

Now, reader, when you shall read what may follow —when you shall hear Paul and Peter talking about slavery, you will please remember that it is not American but Roman slavery. That which could claim a more honorable paternity; growing out of the law of nations, viz: "might gives right," and when might changed sides, the parties changed sides, and the present masters by the same law were the slaves. This, hard as it was, was yet more honorable than that originated in skulking, kidnapping, and piracy. It was not possible for heathenism to originate a system that would equal ours in enormity. There is an intricacy and complexity connected with this, to which Roman slavery was a stranger. The legal restraints and embarrassments imposed upon manumission have bound both the master and the slave. And as the "sweetest wine makes the sourest vinegar," so slavery by the so called christian nations, will, upon the same principle, be the most crafty, subtle, base, and most difficult to uproot.

"Art thou called, being a servant, care not for it: for if thou mayest be made free, use it rather." 1 Cor. vii: 21. There *was* then such a thing as slaves being "made free" in Paul's time. The will of the master was all that was wanting, and the slave *was* "free." But an American slave *can not* be made "free." If the master manumits, he must at the same time give bail for the good behavior of the freed man, or within a given number of days the slave must leave the State, or be sold to the highest bidder in behalf of the State. No matter what his attachments are to the land of his nativity; no matter if his father, mother, brother, sisters, wife, and children are there, he must leave or enter slavery again. Such freedom! ! If Paul were here he would not insult American slaves by saying what he said to slaves in Greece, "if thou mayest be made free," etc.

"Art thou called, being a servant, care not for it." I marvel at the ease with which the apologists of slavery can pass over this passage of Scripture. They say, "Be not perplexed about it;" that is only the same idea with another dress. Art thou called, converted, being a husband, a wife, a father, a mother, a son, or a daughter, be not perplexed about it. To stand in any of these relations is rather afflictive, but being in this *fix* now, make the best of it; "care not for it." Either of these would imply that there was something hard or afflictive in the relation. A kind mother just now said to her dear little one, who unfortunately got one of its fingers badly pinched when shutting the door, "Don't cry, 'care not for it, care not for it,' do not be perplexed about it," are the same forms of speech and sayings used for the same purpose, viz: to comfort in hard allotments, and to express sympathy for the sufferer. "Care not for it;" to lay it to heart will not mend the matter so long as you stand in this relation; but see here, may not your state be changed? "If thou mayest be made free use it rather." To desire freedom is right, and obtain freedom if you can. "If thou mayest be made free," etc. The apostle is not in this place teaching duty, but what is here said bears directly upon relation. No good man will encourage the dissolving of right and justifiable relations; while every good man would say to such as were coerced into a wrong relation—a relation which had a tendency to oppression and injustice—get out of it if you can, do not continue in it if you "may be made free." No language could more unequivocally express the wrongfulness of a relation than to say to the suffering party in that relation, "If thou mayest be made free use it rather;" but, as the chances to be made free were quite uncertain, the apostle said to the suffering christian slave, if, in your civil relations you are a slave, in your moral relations, in your relations to Jesus Christ, you are "free." "He that is called being a servant is the Lord's free man." Ver. 22. The Lord's free man; this was some consolation; man's slave, this was hard—"Ye (christians) are bought with a price, be not ye the servants (slaves) of man." This language is imperative; if it is not, "be of good cheer;" John xvi: 35, is not, "be strong in the Lord;" Eph. vi: 10, is not, "be baptized;" Acts x: 48, is not. Pro-Slavery pleaders slide over this prohibitory command with admirable facility. They say the apostle *only* gave a preference to freedom. Well, this was something against slavery—themselves being judges. But *they* give their preference for slavery, and yet claim Paul as one of their religious advisers under Jesus Christ—claim to have been converted to God by that Gospel Paul preached; they and their leader differ in their preferences. He preferred freedom; they slavery. It is presumable, however, only when it is theirs to be master and somebody else to be the slave. If they had to be the slaves they might readily be converted to the apostle's *preference;* but we deny that the text, "be not ye the slaves of men," simply expresses a preference. What? an inspired apostle having and expressing only a preference in reference to an institution of the gravest importance; so regarded in all ages, and by all men, whether "bond" or "free?" an institution positively right or positively wrong, a positive good or a positive evil? What an insult to Paul; what slander upon the spirit of wisdom and righteousness by which he wrote. They want to make Paul a kind of *go-between*, as many of them are, to hide their own cowardly neutrality under apostolic authority. No, Paul was not the man to set upon two stools; he said to the church members, "*Be not ye the slaves of men*," and by fair implication be not ye the masters of "men," for the one implies the other. When he said to the members of the church, "Be strong in the Lord," and the power of his "might;" "put on the armor of God," etc., he expressed more than a mere preference for strong christians. But to expose this *Pro-slavery* sophism to the weakest reader, we will have another parallel from Paul.

"Be not ye therefore partakers with them." Eph. v: 7. Above are enumerated "fornication, uncleanness, covetousness, filthiness, foolish talking, jesting," etc. "Let no man deceive you with vain words, because of these things cometh the wrath of God upon the children of disobedience." Verse 6th. Then comes the prohibitory command, "Be not ye therefore partakers with them." "For ye were sometimes darkness, but now are ye light in the Lord, walk as the children of the light." Ver. 8th. *I prefer* that ye should no longer be partakers with them. But *I* don't care much either way. "Let no man deceive you with vain words." If then, "Be not ye therefore partakers with them" is a command, "Be ye not the slaves of men" is also a command. Both are in the imperative mood and in the passive voice, and command that certain things should not be done. "Be not fornicators," etc., "Be ye not the slaves of men." But it will be asked, did not the apostle command that every man should abide in the same calling in which he was when converted? Yes, brethren, "let every man wherein he was called therein abide with God." With this exception, however, Paul would say if the converted slaves *can* be made free, let him no longer abide in slavery; "If thou mayest be made free, use it rather." Surely the apostle did not command the slave in the 21st verse to abandon his calling, if he had an opportunity, and in the 24th verse command him to abide in it. This, then, is an exceptional case. But as to all the other callings or relations inquired after, (see verses 1st to 29th, inclusive,) let these remain as they were then called. The sum of the apostle's answer to the church's inquiry in regard to slavery was this, let the relation be dissolved when it can be, "if thou mayest be made free," etc. Let not the relation be extended. Let not the free, by any act or will of their own, become slaves, "ye are bought with a price; be ye not the slaves of men; ye are called in freedom, abide in freedom; ye were not masters when called, then abide as you are, do not become masters, with the aforesaid exception, brethren, let every man wherein he was called therein abide with God; let the relation of master and slave be dissolved so far as the present masters will consent; and to the rest of you, brethren, I say abide as you are." We appeal to the laws of language, to logic, and to every correct principle of interpretation for the correctness of this view of the passage. We challenge criticism. If slaveholders could find commands as unequivocal for the continuance of slavery in the church, as these bearing directly upon the abolition of it in the church, they might with much assurance appeal to Paul and Peter for authority.

As the passage examined is the only one in the New Testament bearing upon the abstract question of relation, and as it has been twisted and perverted to subserve *pro-slavery* ends, we have been at some pains to wrest it from such prostitution.

If the Apostles so regulated the duties of master and slave that when the specified duties were discharged, the relation would be fostered and continued in the church, then might our opponents claim apostolic favor in behalf of the relation; but the most artful apologists have to concede too much to set up such a claim.

There is now before me the most ingeniously written apology for American Slavery that has yet come under my observation. We shall give a few extracts. A. C. Review, edited and published by Benjamin Franklin, vol. 1st, No. 2, page 39: "Men whose hearts become largely imbued with the spirit of the Gospel, gradually relax the bonds; the converted servant becomes better, and the feeling of kindness between master and slave is increased, and in thousands of instances results in his emancipation. In this way the peaceable, orderly, and legitimate workings of the religion of Jesus Christ have legally emancipated more slaves, in these United States," etc. That such was the effect of christianity upon Roman Slavery is a well authenticated fact—that such would be its influence upon American Slavery we doubt not—that such is its influence we deny. Where is the evidence that through the influence of christianity, "thousands of slaves are being emancipated in 'these United States.'" We will not charge the writer with exaggeration, but we do think there is too much of the *hyperbole* about this for sober fact. But in the next sentence he makes large abatements, and says: "Hundreds of good men, (and of these good men he names but two,) one is no more, the other is yet living, these yielding to that preference the bible gives freedom over slavery in the emancipation of all the slaves that fell into their hands. Such men show their faith by legal, good, and peaceable works of righteousness." Whether a philosopher would smile or frown at this, would, I imagine, depend upon the amount of reverence he had for the Bible. Two good men, A. Campbell and B. W. Stone, have shown their "faith by legal, good, and peaceable works of righteousness in the emancipation of their slaves." Their faith in what? Their "faith in the preference the Bible gives freedom over slavery." The legitimate inference from these facts is, that a good man's preferences will agree with Bible preferences, and such will show their faith by corresponding works. Why not insist upon this, Bro. Franklin, that all the "good" slaveholders in the church must do as these have done. That, as the "Bible gives a preference to freedom over slavery, so all "good men" must give the same preference, and make their preference manifest by "emancipating" all their slaves. Bro. Franklin says of the Bible upon this subject: "Here we plant our foot." *This is well.* When you next write upon this subject, cite your readers in the South to those passages in the Bible where God has "preferences for freedom over slavery," and then call their attention to those good men, and say to those slaveholders who will not emancipate their slaves—who have not as yet followed the example of these "good men," "remember those who have spoken to you the word of God!" whose faith follow considering the end of their behavior. Brother Franklin, you should do this, or you should take your "foot" from the Bible, and your *hand* likewise. Moreover, this would do more good than your fine declamation about abolitionists making the *Church* a political *engine.* But we must say a little more about this "Bible preference for freedom over slavery." Prefer means to regard something more than something else, a choice—as, this is good but that is better. There are such preferences in the Bible as "the eating of meats and the observance of days." "He that giveth her in marriage doeth well, but he that giveth her not in marriage doeth better." If the Bible, the exponent of the will of God to man, has placed slavery in this category, these apologists, these pliant writers are right enough. Then we will say slavery is good, but freedom is better. If such were my understanding, if I could so classify slavery, I would never have troubled myself about it. We do, then, regard the word "preference" as a mere salvo—an evasion—an artful sophism, most dishonorable to God, who looks upon the quality of things, who once said to slaveholders, "Let the oppressed go free," "break every yoke," and now says to the Church, "Ye are bought with a price, be ye not the slaves of men." And finally on the question of relation—the relation is to the institution what the foundation is to the building—if that be substantial the structure may be permanent—if the basis is defective the building can not stand, *but* by the aid of *braces, props, etc.* If the relation of master and slave is right, the abuse of the relation can form no valid objection to the relation. That which is of *itself wrong* and *faulty*, can not be *abused*. To say the thing is abused, is to pronounce the highest encomium upon its intrinsic excellence. When husbands and wives, parents and children "become largely imbued with the spirit of the Gospel," the parties in these relations are made better, the "feelings of kindness" between husband and wife are "increased," and the relation becomes the more indissoluble. Is not this true with reference to all parties in right relations? It is true.

How strange that, after brother F. had put forth his strong hand to support the tottering fabric, after he had driven away the mischievous abolitionists from the temple of slavery, he should have uttered the sentence quoted. "Men whose hearts become largely imbued with the spirit of the Gospel, gradually relax the bonds, the converted servant becomes better, and the feeling of kindness between the master and slave is increased, and in thousands of instances results in his emancipation."

Whether intended or unintended, this is an assault upon the rightfulness of the slave relation, for which the editor of the Review can make no amends to slaveholders.

When the "spirit of the Gospel has largely imbued the heart of the master and the heart of the slave," the tendency is to separate, to dissolve the relation; but the absence of the "spirit of the Gospel" tends to unite and sustain the relation of master and slave. In all lawful, domestic, social, and religious relations the spirit of the Gospel *draws:* but in this it *drives.* Like the centripetal and centrifugal forces in nature.

the one attracting and the other repelling. So soon, then, as "the spirit of the Gospel shall have largely imbued the hearts" of all slaveholders, slavery will be brought to a perpetual end. I believe it with all my heart, dear brother.

If the spirit of the Gospel, which is but another word for the "spirit of Christ," will promote the emancipation of slaves, slavery must be an evil, for the good spirit of Christ will not destroy good. But when the "spirit of holiness" is brought to bear upon evil, the evil will be "overcome" by the "good." This is a *truism of universal application.*

But as long as the leaders of the people say *Slavery is good,* "both Bible and Testament, Moses and Paul, admit and sustain the relation of bond-master and bond-servant for life;" and as this is believed by masters and slaves, it will be difficult—most difficult—to "imbue their hearts with the spirit of the Gospel," for, but few, if any, will understand the mystery, how the Gospel can both "admit and sustain the relation of master and slave for life," and at the same time influence the master, "largely imbued with the spirit of the Gospel," to emancipate all his slaves that may fall into his hands, as brother B. says two "good men" have done.

But here is something hard for the unlearned to understand, how a "good man" can refuse to "sustain that which both Moses and Paul do admit and sustain." Be that as it may, we rejoice in this, that the aforesaid living "good man" did what he knew both Moses and Paul would justify, and "emancipated all the slaves that fell into his hands." In this he has "shown his faith by legal, good, and peaceable works of righteousness," his position to the contrary notwithstanding.

We feel strongly impressed with the conviction that all good men will do likewise.

ESSAY VI.

My last was devoted mainly to the relation of master and servant, as disapproved by the apostle in his instructions to the Church of Corinth. "Art thou called, being a servant, care not for it, for if thou mayest be made free, use it rather." "Ye are bought with a price, be not ye the servants (slaves) of men."

In ethics, relation precedes duty. To prescribe duty, is not necessarily an approval of the relation, as we have shown in a previous article. The reader will bear in mind, that while the apostle gave commands to both slaves and masters, that God neither originated or approved the relation, for he never commissioned one Gentile nation to make war with another, and for the conquerers to enslave the conquered. Whatever commission God gave the Jews in a given case, as his executives, has nothing to do with this discussion.

God has given his sanction to civil government, but for the strong to oppress the "weak," is not government, but oppression, a perversion, an abuse of government. God approves the civil magistrate *only* so far as he is a "terror to evil doers, and a praise to those that do well." The enslavement of the weaker party by the stronger among the Gentiles never was a "terror to evil doers," because, never commanded by God as punishment for crime. Therefore when an apostle of Jesus Christ was writing to those coerced into the relation of slaves, a relation that originated in brute force, he said, let this relation be abolished; "if thou mayest be made free," etc.

Next in order then, is duty. "Servants, be subject to your masters with all fear; not only to the good and gentle but also to the froward," 1st Peter, ii: 18.

1st. Who is the writer? 2d. Who is he writing to? 3d. What is he writing for? Peter, an apostle, therefore an ambassador for Christ, was the writer of this quotation. The persons written to were christians, but in their civil relations they were slaves. The object of the writer was to teach these Disciples of Christ their duties to their masters, and to God, also to reconcile them to their suffering condition. This epistle is general, but contains specific instructions to particular classes. From the 18th verse to the 25th inclusive of the 2nd chapter, is to slaves. From the 1st verse to the 6th of the 3rd chapter, inclusive, is to wives. The 7th verse is to husbands. The 8th verse is the beginning of an address to all. These are appropriated teachings, and will apply to no others, only as the circumstances of others and theirs are similar. That which was intended by the writer for "servants," was addressed to "servants." "Servants, be subject," etc. "Likewise ye wives." "Likewise ye husbands." "Finally, be ye all of one mind." These things premised, we will go into a brief analysis of Peter's address to "servants." "Servants, be subject to your masters with all fear; not only to the good and gentle, but also to the froward." v: 18. This is a precept, and as plain *as* precept. For this is thankworthy; if a man for conscience toward God endure grief, suffering wrongfully. For what glory is it when you are buffeted for your faults, ye shall take it patiently, but if when you do well, and take it patiently, this is acceptable with God, (ver. 19, 20.) This is exhortation, or motive to the discharge of duty. But it also leads out the real condition of slaves, viz: that they are exposed to "grief," to suffer "wrongfully" and from conscience to God, they should patiently submit to the wrongs incident to their condition as slaves. "For even hereunto were ye (ye slaves) called." What were they called unto? to be christians? no, but to suffer patiently the wrongs, the trials, to which their condition subjected them, "because Christ also suffered for *us*," leaving *us* in general, an example. That *ye* (slaves in particular) should follow his steps; who did no sin, neither was guile found in his mouth; and yet he suffered. His condition like yours, exposed Him to maltreatment and to suffering. But as He was a passive, non-resisting sufferer, so be ye;" who, when he was reviled, reviled not again, when He suffered, He threatened not, but committed Himself to him that judgeth righteously." There was no redress for his grievances before the court of the Jews, or the court of the Gentiles. His rights were invaded and trodden under foot. Even one of his judges said to his accusers, I find no fault in him, John xix: 4. But notwithstanding, he was "crucified." What now was to be done? Thanks be to God, there is yet another judge, and another court besides the *corrupt* courts of this world. Jesus Christ, who is here set before the suffering christian slave for his imitation, "committed *himself* to him, that judgeth righteously." Caiaphas, the High Priest, said "he is worthy of death." Pilate, the Roman Procurator, said "take ye him and crucify *him*; for I find no fault in him." But Jesus Christ took an *appeal* from these judges, to that Judge that "judgeth righteously." He redressed his wrongs, reversed his sentence. God the righteous judge raised him from the dead, took him to heaven, sent his spirit to the world, to be his advocate on earth.

The points of the coincidence, between Jesus Christ and slaves, are; 1st. His condition in this world exposed him to unjust suffering. The condition of Roman slaves exposed them to "grief, suffering wrongfully." Jesus Christ could have no redress of his grievances before the judges of this world. Slaves had no legal rights. Their only bill of rights was the will of their owners, liable to be the sport of passion, to all who might find them at home or abroad, to be whipped or murdered, without sympathy or redress. The hurt to a slave was estimated as the hurt done to a brute. 3rd. Jesus Christ was put to death for no offense. Judge Pilate said three times to his accusers, "I find no fault in him," and yet he said "take and crucify him." He was crucified because he was in the power of his enemies. "For though he was crucified through weakness, yet he liveth by the power of God." 2 Cor. xiii: 4. Roman slaves were frequently butchered by hundreds and by thousands, as the mere occasion of youthful frolic. Being unprotected by the government, they were put to death through weakness. 4th. Christ was crucified. Slaves were usually crucified. These are some of the historical points of sameness between Jesus Christ and slaves. Well did Paul say, "he took on him the form of a servant." On account of this similarity, the apostle referred converted slaves to their patient redeemer for example. He was "reviled," ye are "reviled," follow his "example," "revile not again." He "suffered," ye "suffer," follow his "steps," threaten not. He was bought, and he was sold, ye are bought and sold. He was "striped," ye are striped, "by whose stripes ye are healed." He bore stripes patiently for you. Do ye bear "stripes" patiently for his sake. "For this is thankworthy," etc. "For ye were as sheep going astray, but are now returned to the shepherd and Bishop of your souls." No one cared for your souls. Jesus Christ is now your "shepherd," he will protect you, he is the "Bishop of your souls," he has espoused your cause; refer your "griefs" to him, he will make it all right with you.

Pro-slavery critics say the word that means slave in the original text, is also applied to Jesus Christ; I believe it, for he "came not to be ministered unto, but to minister." "But made himself of no reputation, (slaves have no reputation,) and took on him the form of a servant," Phil. ii: 7. This was necessary that his humiliation on earth might be complete. Suppose, if such a thing had been possible, he had made himself *of* reputation, and had taken the form of a *slave master*, what then? we would answer almost in the cry of one of old, "Wo! to the world, and wo! to myself."

The words "Bishop of your souls," close Peter's address to servants (slaves). The next class is to wives, "Likewise, ye wives," etc. If the condition of slaves called forth such sympathy and compassion, who will say that the apostle admitted and sustained a relation that inflicted such "griefs" and "sufferings" upon unoffending men and women?

When Peter said to servants, "servants, be subject to," etc., would the "servants" addressed conclude from what follows, that the apostle approved the relation of master and servant, and sympathized with them because of their happy condition, and sought to reconcile them to a right relation, and the happy circumstances growing out of said relation, by referring them to their suffering Savior for an example of patience? If Peter intended to impress the slaves with a sense of their enslavement being right, he was most unfortunate in this address, and must have failed in his object; but if he intended to reconcile them to their hard allotments, that they might bear the sorrows incident to their condition with patience, his address was admirably calculated to secure his object.

"Servants, be obedient to them that are your masters, according to the flesh, with fear and trembling, in singleness of heart, as unto Christ; not with eye service as men-pleasers, but as the servants of Christ, doing the will of God from the heart: with good will doing service, as to the Lord, and not to men;" etc. "And ye masters, do the same thing unto them, forbearing threatening; knowing that your master, also, is in heaven; neither is there respect of persons with him." Eph. 6th chap. That any relation may be perpetuated, the duties must be in harmony with the relation. Parents, "*obey*" your children, would subvert the relation in all its practical phases. "And the" husband "*see*" that he "reverence" his wife. This change in duty would so affect the relation as to extinguish it altogether.

The apostle so regulated the duties of master and slave, that when discharged the relation was extinct. This is our affirmation.

"And, ye masters, do the same things unto them. What are the "same things?" Above, the apostle required servants to do "the will of God from the heart," in respect to their masters. Masters, do the same, "the will of God from the heart," as it respects your servants, "*forbearing threatening*," this was the "will of God."

To menace, to denounce, to terrify by words, is the mildest form of slave chastisement. If the "will of God" disallowed "threatening," it surely would not allow the more severe forms of corporal punishment, *such* as are usually inflicted upon slaves. Let slave discipline be abolished, and the system is abolished. That which originates in *violence*, can only be sustained by *violence*. Let whipping, manacling, burning, hanging for misdemeanors, and forcible recapture, be abandoned, and slavery is among the things that were. "Forbearing threatening, knowing that your master also is in heaven." Let the master be influenced by the fear of God, and the chattel feature is no more. The property element is the vitalizing spirit of the system. Let a man realize that he has a "master in heaven," and he can no more sell his fellow-man into perpetual slavery, than he could sell himself.

"Knowing that your master also, is in heaven: neither is there respect of persons with him." "Respect of persons," is to slavery what the corner-stone is to a building, or, what the key-stone is to the arch. The Romans said their slaves were of "*mean birth*," of "servile birth," of "disingenuous birth." Americans say, their slaves are the descendants of "Ham," and that "Ham" means "black," and the negroes are "black," and that God doomed these "blacks" to be slaves. Others say that they are of inferior "creation," not "human," not "men," naturally "mean," will "lie" and "steal," can't "take care of themselves," those "born of slave women," are of mean "birth," slave mothers have no affection for their "children," it don't hurt them to sell their "babies," as it does the white "mothers." This is a specimen of pro-slavery parlance, the unhallowed assumption that "God is a respecter of persons." "Neither is there respect of persons with him." Slaveholders do not believe this, not a word of it; they believe that God made their slaves to be slaves, and that they have a right to use them for the purpose for which God made them. The accidents of birth, of country, or of color, have no influence upon God. All can see the bearing of the doctrine that "God is no respecter of persons" upon slavery.

The principle contained in this quotation carried out, slavery can not exist. If Paul had intended the continuance of slavery in the church of Ephesus, he would not have said to the masters, "forbear threatening," you "have a master in heaven," "with him is no respect of persons." In no slave-code under heaven, are such duties and considerations enjoined upon masters. Duties incompatible with slavery, and when discharged it is no more slavery.

"Masters, give to your slaves that which is just and

equal, knowing that ye also have a master in heaven." Cor. iv: 1. This reading suggests an important inquiry, viz: by what standard was the required "justice" and "equality," to be determined? If, by our slave-laws, food, raiment, lodging, shelter, medicine when sick, would be giving what was "just and equal." No compensation for labor, no education in this bill of rights. To sell the husband, the wife, the children—to separate as far as the extremes of slave territory, to inflict corporal punishment, etc., are neither injustice nor inequality according to this standard. If the Roman slave-code was the rule of measurement, then, the will of the master, be the same more or less, was "justice and equality." Justice and equality, between man and man, differ as the moral standards vary in different countries. When a man deals with his neighbor according to the laws of the community, he has done all that can be required of him as a citizen, however he may have injured or oppressed his neighbor. The rule of equity in this case, "masters, give to your servants that which is just and equal," was either the *law* of the State, or the *law* of Christ; Roman (heathen) morality, or christian morality. If the former, the *will* of the master, however his *will* might be influenced by interest or passion, was the slave's *only* bill of rights.

You say not the former but the latter, the *law* of Christ—the morality taught by Jesus Christ and his Apostles. But might not the following be the rule of equity in this case? "What, with all the premises known to yourself, you consider to be just and equitable." Millennial Harbinger for August 1854. This exposition is in keeping with every slave-code, ancient and modern. "What, with all the premises known to *yourself*, you consider to be just and equitable." This leaves the rights of christian slaves in the church, precisely as they were in the State, to be meted and measured by the will of the master. The master is answerable to no law. His own judgment of what is equitable between him and his slaves, is the law of right.

Suppose then a master, a member of the congregation in Bethany, Virginia, should be accused of having cruelly whipped his slave, or any other maltreatment, might he not say, brethren, I did what, with all the premises before me, I knew to be right? Or, suppose the accusation were for withholding food, raiment, or medicine, would not *defendant* say, brethren, I gave my slave what " with all the premises before me I consider to be just and equitable?" The Bishop of the congregation would probably say to the accusers, there is no cause of action, the brother is only exercising his rightful *prerogative* over his servant. Such would be, and such are the practical workings of the interpretation given by the Harbinger.

With such interpretations of the divine teachings, slaveholders can not be the subjects of discipline, as it respects their slaves — *a good reason why they are not.*

To arrive at correct conclusions, with respect to the meaning of the text, "masters, give," etc., we must first inquire, in what relation did christian slaves stand to christian masters; " For by one spirit are we all baptized into one body," " whether we be bond or free." 1st Cor. xii: 13. " One is your master, even Christ, and ye are brethren." This was something different from the State. In the State they were proprietors and chattels, in the church they were brethren. Would the old duties be in harmony with the new relation? They would not. Would justice and equality be the same in the church as in the State? "Justice" and "equality," between the proprietor and his property—nonsense. The demand for justice and equality in the church must mean justice and equality according to the moral standard of the church. Now, if the church has but one moral standard, and that is applicable to all, then the existence of slavery in primitive times, was only nominal in the church, not *real.* Do we find in the New Testament, one law for the free *members*, and another for the *bond* members? Let the rights guaranteed to the free citizens of any slave State be applied to the slaves, and whatever the condition of the slaves may be, they are *no* longer slaves. They might be still under the yoke nominally for a time, but their freedom would be as certain as the shining out of the sun when the clouds have removed. One law based upon equity, claiming equal rights for all, must remove all the distinctions, save the natural and official. The distinctions created by slavery, in the Roman empire, were artificial, arbitrary, and unnatural. Such distinctions can only be kept up by a special legislation, arranged with reference to this specific object. Strike down the law of primogeniture, and you strike down the distinction between the English Nobility and Peasantry. Let all be "equally" eligible to be promoted to stations of honor and trust, upon the ground of merit and competency, and you create one "equal" political brotherhood.

If, therefore, Paul used the words "just" and

"equal," in an appropriated sense, in the case of slaves, as meaning *less* than their current import, then is christianity a system of *tyranny* and *despotism*. If this be so, we must understand and apply such scriptures as the following, in a limited sense, when applied to slaves. "Render therefore to all their dues." "Honor all men." "Therefore, all things whatsoever ye would that men should do unto you, do ye even so unto them, for this is the law and the prophets." The master must fix the limitations, and his own judgment, "with all the premises before him," will decide how much *less* is "due" to his slave brother, than to his free brother, both as it respects his wife, his children, or compensation for his labor, and his *own* decision in the case would be final. The master too would decide how much less of "honor" was "due" to his slave brother, simply because a tyrannical government had made him his slave, perhaps, to say the least of it, as aged, as pious, as virtuous, as learned as himself. Whatever abatements he would make in the practical application of these moral precepts to his slaves, would also be made by the other members of the church.

That unerring rule of right enforced by Jesus Christ upon his disciples, "All things whatsoever ye would that men should do unto you, do ye even so unto them," was a dead letter between the christian master and his slave, or, it meant *less*, between the master and his slaves, than between other parties. When Paul commanded masters to give their servants what was "just" and "equal," this precept was not to be taken into the account, or, not applied as between other parties, on questions of "justice" and "equality." Nay, what with all the premises known to yourself, you consider to be "just" and "equitable," "so hermeneutics and logic decide," says the Harbinger. Why not say "so" Jesus Christ and his apostles "decide." They do not so "decide," "hermeneutics and logic" to the contrary notwithstanding. But the following is their decision on all questions of right between brethren: "That no man go beyond, and defraud his brother in any matter; because that the Lord is the avenger of all such, as we also have forewarned you and testified." 1 Thes. iv: 6. They claim justice and "equity" for every brother and in every thing. That no man "*defraud* his brother in *any matter!*"

In the New Testament we have but one law, and that law is applied to all its subjects; no favoritism, no partiality in its application. "I charge thee before God, and the Lord Jesus Christ, and the elect angels, that thou observe these things without preferring one before another, doing nothing by partiality." This is Paul's logic. This is Paul's sense of "just" and "equal," no "respect of persons," no personal preference, no partiality, what is "due" to one christian brother is "due" to another, according to the law of love. "Be ye all of one mind, love as brethren, be pitiful, be courteous."

"Justice" and "equality" between the master and servant was not required by the State. If Paul required more than the State, we shall submit the question to the Harbinger or the American Christian Review, to say how much more. Until better informed, we shall understand Paul to have required "masters" to give to their servants in all things precisely what they would give others in their employ, and subject to their command, neither more nor less.

The doctrine that Jesus Christ, the "one Lord" of the "one body," would authorize one class of his subjects to enrich themselves at the expense of another class, because a despotic government had placed them in their power, is to make christian morality no better than heathen morality.

The man that so reads and understands the teachings of Jesus Christ and his inspired Apostles, must look at them through slaveholders' glasses, as the writer once looked at the Bible through Calvinistic glasses, and every chapter was full of Calvinism.

We have in this article examined three passages. The first addressed to slaves *only*, the others to masters and slaves. The duties enjoined differ not from the duties in general, and commanded to all. That christians should bear ill-treatment with patience—that those in the service of others should be faithful—that those in authority should "forbear threatening," menacing language, that they should bear in mind that God did not respect their persons, because they exercised rule, but should rule in the fear of the Lord. In these there is nothing peculiar.

Masters, give to your servants that which is just and equal, has, I believe, no parallel. But its novelty consists in form only. It differs not in meaning from this, "render to all their dues." There was no occasion for this form of address in any other case. Where there is a contract, payment is required as *per* agreement. But there being no contract in this case, Paul, an apostle of Jesus Christ, *in the name of Christ*, espoused the cause of the servant, and demanded for him, and in his behalf, what was "just" and "equal," not as for a servant, but above a "servant, a brother beloved." Under such regulations slavery could not exist. It would be as easy to conceive how the rudest barbarism could exist under the highest and most refined state of civilization, as for slavery to exist in the apostolic churches, under the direction of apostolic teaching. There is more than one way of killing an evil. There is more than one way of killing a wolf. You may kill him as certainly by starvation as by beheading. Let slaves become unprofitable to their masters, and they will soon abandon the system. Let the right of selling be denied to the masters, and they will quit breeding them. Let compensation for their labor be exacted according to equal standards of appreciation, and they would soon prefer free labor.

"Masters, give to your servants that which is just and equal," "just, upright, equitable." One of the canonized principles of interpretation among our brethren is this, viz., that the inspired writers used language in its current meaning. By the application of this rule, they have accomplished much toward making the divine word intelligible. Does the word "just" in this place mean less than its current value? If so, the qualification should have accompanied the requisition; candor would require this. "If the trumpet gives an uncertain sound, who shall prepare himself for the battle?" Give him what is "just" according to all the "premises." But what are the premises? The master is the master, and the slave is the slave. These are the "premises." The relation was approved in the State, and it is "admitted and sustained" in the

Church. Does this belong to the "premises" too? Yes; but not to Paul's "premises." For he said to the slave members of the church, "if thou mayest be free, use it rather."

Now what are Paul's premises? If your christian master will not make you "free" he must give you what is "just and equal." These are Paul's "premises" and conclusions. As an ambassador for Christ, he claimed for the servant that which is just and equal, namely, that christian masters must give their slaves what will make them equal to other slaves, "equal" in a comparative sense. That is, they must give them what slaves usually receive at the hands of their masters, or, in other words, christian masters must give their servants as much as heathen masters give their servants. This would have been "equal" like others, as the word imports. But where is the net gain to the converted slave? Ah, that is the question. "Equal," then, according to the usages of the church, namely, what other christian masters give their servants. But this implies that there was some kind of conventional agreement with masters as to what would be "just" in the case of slaves. Say justice to a hired-servant would be to pay him, for his labor, as *per* contract, to let him appropriate his own earnings, to let him own himself, his wife, and children. But, justice to a slave-servant was less than this. If less, then this class of servants were a class by themselves to whom the word "just," in its common acceptation, would not apply. If then one master gave to his servants what other masters gave their servants, he gave them what was "just and equal." This rule of equality was special, to be applied only to this specific class of church members. If there was in apostolic times an act of special legislation, to meet this particular case, we ask, where is it? we ask for chapter and verse. "Equality" in morals is to make one "equal" to another in his personal rights. The word equal is always used in a comparative sense:

> "With equal love their spirits flame;
> The same their joy, their song the same."

The question to be decided, is simply this, who are in the comparison? "Masters, give to your servants that which is just and equal."

Here is the issue. The pro-slavery party assume, that the comparison is between heathen and christian masters and their slaves. In the light of this assumption, what has Paul accomplished for the slave? Just what we see in these United States,—left the slave subject to the will of his master; a chattel in every sense of the word; to be treated as a chattel by his master; to be treated by his master's creditors as a chattel; to be treated by the State as a chattel. *Glorious "justice" and "equality!"*

We assume that the comparison is not between masters, but between dependents; that this class of dependents should receive what was "just" and what would make them "equal" to other dependents, in all the rights of humanity and religion, as ordained by the gospel of Christ.

The consideration enforced upon the master, "knowing that ye also have a master in heaven," gives strength to this conclusion. Would the masters be "equal" to other saints in all the gracious rights of the gospel, then let them extend the same "equal" rights to their subordinates. Aside from the plain obvious import of the text, this interpretation does honor to Jesus Christ, does honor to Paul, and does something toward bettering the condition of the slave. The state had robbed him of his God-given rights, but christianity gave them back to him again, by claiming in his behalf what was "just and equal" according to the same law of moral right applicable to all the members of the church. More can not be claimed for any individual, in any organization, secular or religious, than justice and equality. And when Paul exacted this from masters, in the most unqualified sense, he could do no more for any christian brother, in any relation, who had been deprived of personal rights.

Moreover the command, Masters, give to your servants that which is "just and equal," implies, that hitherto they had not received what was "just and equal" in the State, but in the church masters must give their servants what was just and equal, or else make them "free." To give them what was "just and equal," was only another way to make them "free," not so summarily to be sure, as the usual form of manumission, but no less certain. As certain as the command, "Fathers, provoke not your children to anger, but bring them *up* in the nurture and admonition of the Lord," would put an end to the barbarous practice of exposing infants.

ESSAY VII.

We shall now examine Paul to Timothy, 1st Epistle, 6th chapter, to the 11th verse inclusive.

"Let as many servants as are under the yoke, count their own masters worthy of all honor, that the name of God and his doctrine be not blasphemed. And they that have believing masters, let them not despise *them* because they are brethren; but rather do them service, because they are faithful and beloved partakers of the benefit.

"These things teach and exhort.

"If any man teach otherwise, and consent not to wholesome words, even the words of our Lord Jesus Christ, and to the doctrine which is according to godliness, he is proud, knowing nothing, but doting about questions and strifes of words, whereof cometh envy, strife, railings, evil surmisings.

"Perverse disputings of men of corrupt minds, and destitute of truth, supposing that gain is godliness; from such withdraw thyself.

"But godliness with contentment is great gain.

"For we brought nothing into this world, and it is certain we can carry nothing out.

"And having food and raiment, let us be therewith content.

"But they that will be rich fall into temptation and a snare, and *into* many foolish and hurtful lusts, which drown men in destruction and perdition.

"For the love of money is the root of all evil; which while some coveted after, they have erred from the faith, and pierced themselves through with many sorrows."

This is one unbroken connection, therefore this extract entire has some bearing upon slavery. The 11th verse changes the subject: "But thou, O man of God, flee these things."

From this passage it is quite evident, that there was a controversy pending upon the subject of slavery in the church at Ephesus, and Paul was giving direction to Timothy as to the true issue, and the standard to which the question in debate should be submitted; that this question, then agitating the church, should be brought to the same *umpire* to which all questions that had, or might unsettle the peace of the church. Where there is no authority, there can be neither reference, nor decision. In all organizations there must be some standard authority, to which differing parties may appeal as the end of "strife."

In our civil relations, we refer our differences to the wholesome words of the statute book, and the "doctrine" which is according to Blackstone. Some refer their religious strife to the wholesome words of John Calvin and the "doctrine" which is according to the Confession of Faith. Others to the wholesome words of John Wesley and the doctrine of the Discipline. When the standard authorities have given their verdict, the controversy is settled. In the Epistles of the Apostles we find frequent references to that which was authority in the primitive church. "Now, I beseech you, brethren, mark them which cause divisions and offenses, contrary to the doctrine which ye have learned, and avoid them." Rom. xvi: 17. "As I besought thee to abide still at Ephesus, when I went into Macedonia, that thou mightest charge some that they teach no other doctrine." 1st Tim. i: 3

"Teach no other doctrine," is, however, quite indefinite. But the allusion must have been understood. So intelligible was this form of speech: "other doctrine, doctrine which ye have not learned," that a reference was all-sufficient.

On the subject of Slavery some were teaching another "doctrine," a "doctrine" which the church had not "learned" from Jesus Christ and his Apostles.

Therefore, "if any man teach otherwise and consent not to wholesome words, *even* the words of the Lord Jesus Christ, and the doctrine which is according to godliness, he is proud, knowing nothing," etc. We do not here affirm on which side of the question these "proud" know nothings were, whether *pro* or *anti*, but only affirm that the "wholesome words of Christ, and the doctrine which is according to godliness," was the theological standard, by which all question of order, morality, and piety were determined. This is the only authoritative standard in christianity. All others are human, and therefore not decisive on any question of gospel truth and christian duty. The wholesome words of our Lord Jesus Christ must have been words uttered by himself. His words were again brought to the recollection of the Apostles by the Holy Spirit, according to promise. This had to be, that the Apostles might fulfil their great commission. "All power in heaven and in earth is given unto me," "Go ye, therefore, teach all nations, baptizing them," etc., "teaching them (the baptized) to observe all things whatsoever I have commanded you." The baptized "continued steadfastly in the Apostles' doctrine," etc. Acts 2. The Apostles' doctrine was the all things Jesus Christ had commanded them to observe, and they enjoined the observance of these things upon their converts. The wholesome words (teaching) of our Lord Jesus Christ, was the doctrine of godliness, and the Apostles' doctrine (teaching) was according to this. These things premised, it is in order to inquire, in the next place, upon whom did Paul animadvert, when he said to Timothy: "If any man consent not to wholesome words," etc., "He is proud, knowing nothing, but doting about questions and strifes of words," etc.? This brings the question to a plain issue.

Slaveholders and their friends (apologists) say with great assurance, this was a rebuke to abolitionists.

There were, then, abolitionists in the church in those days. Abolitionism claims an honorable antiquity! That it was a rebuke to *anti*-slavery "teachers," or to *pro*-slavery "teachers," is a clear case. But to which is a question yet to be settled. The pro-slavery application is an assumption, *a reckless assumption*. For this charge we hold ourselves responsible. If we do not make it good let us be corrected, and we will take this back with pleasure. Then, to the work: "If any man teach otherwise, and consent not to wholesome words, *even* the words of our Lord Jesus Christ, and the doctrine which is according to godliness, He is proud, knowing nothing."

Has any pro-slavery D.D. or scribe shown that Roman slavery was "according to the wholesome words of our Lord Jesus Christ, and the doctrine which is according to godliness?" Whatever defence they may have made of the slavery that then agitated the church, has not been upon this basis, namely, "the wholesome words of our Lord Jesus Christ," etc. We call upon them now to prove: 1st, That

Roman slavery was in harmony with the "wholesome words of our Lord Jesus Christ," etc., and 2d, that American slavery is so like Roman slavery, that the "wholesome words" (teachings) of our Lord Jesus Christ will justify the latter as they did the former.

We submit this to our brethren as an overture, and as an end of strife. The logical aspects of the controversy require this. If the stern rebuke "he is proud," etc., means *me*, *I* should and will "repent," nay more, I will *reform*, and I think those of our brethren who are now teaching anti-slavery "doctrine," will confess their wrong, and cease from teaching a "doctrine" contrary to the "wholesome" teachings of Jesus Christ, and the "doctrine which is according to godliness."

Are we not worthy of this effort on your part, or do you look upon us as incorrigible? Your conservativeness will never convince us of our error, if in error we be; neither will your occasional sallies of ridicule and ill-humor turn back the mighty current of anti-slavery sentiment. "Come, then, let us reason together."

Paul commanded Timothy to "withdraw" himself from such as would not "consent to wholesome words, *even* the words of our Lord Jesus Christ, and the doctrine which is according to godliness." Your work is before you. Proceed, then. But you must do better service, than simply to say, that Paul was here chastising abolitionists. We shall require of you, by a fair inductive argument, to show that slavery as it is—as it now is—as it is among us,—is according to the "*words*" of Jesus Christ, and the "Apostles' doctrine." We have, by long and loud profession, adopted these "words" and "doctrine" as our directory—*our only directory* on all questions of morality and piety. Paul said to his son Timothy, let the controversy be brought to this test, and those who will not abide its decision, from such do you "withdraw yourself." Timothy's duty was plain. Our duty is equally so. The controversy is the same. The parties in debate are the same. The authority, by which the difference is to be adjusted, is the same. It only remains to be settled, whether the "wholesome words of our Lord Jesus Christ," "and the doctrine which is according to godliness," are on the side of slavery or on the side of freedom. Here the mind must make a decision. These "words" and "doctrine" can not be on both sides, nor yet neutral, else why refer the issue to them?

We will now, with candor, examine the subject. Verse 1st: "Let as many servants as are under the yoke count their masters worthy of all honor, that the name of God and his doctrine be not blasphemed."

The reader will observe, that the command to the christian servant to "honor" his unbelieving master, is not based upon his duty to his master, because he is his master; but that the servant, by thus "honoring" his unbelieving master, might cause him to honor the "name of God" and his "doctrine." This every christian is required to do: to treat others with respect, whether worthy of respect or not, that they may "*win* them to Christ." To this understanding of the command to servants, "count your own masters worthy of all honor," "the wholesome words of our Lord Jesus Christ" will apply. "Thou shalt love thy neighbor as thyself," will be quite apposite in this case. Did the converted slave prize the salvation of the Gospel for himself, then would he desire the same blessing for his master. He would willingly "honor" him, that he might be instrumental in saving him. Again: "Let your light so shine before men, that they may see your good works, and glorify your Father who is in heaven." Again: "Love your enemies, bless them that curse you, do good to them that hate you," etc., that ye may be the children of your Father who is in heaven." "For if you love them who love you, what reward have you?"

Our space forbids more extracts to this point from the moral lessons taught by Jesus Christ. Every moral principle or duty he taught naturally falls into this view of the subject. The same doctrine pervades all the apostolic teachings. "Walk in wisdom toward them that are without." "This is thankworthy, if a man for conscience toward God endure grief, suffering wrongfully." "Honor all men."

It is, then, according to the "words of our Lord Jesus Christ and the doctrine of godliness," that believing servants should honor their unbelieving masters, with a view to their spiritual and eternal good. But this is no more than christians in general are required to do, *even* towards their enemies.

Now let us look at the other side. The advocates of slavery assume that Paul required servants to "honor" their masters, because they were their masters. And they, the servants, were "under the yoke" —the "yoke" the symbol of oppression. This is the slaveholder's interpretation. But, before this exegesis of the text can be allowed, we must erase the last number of the sentence,—"that the name of God and his doctrine be not blasphemed," must be stricken out. Then the passage would read: "Let as many servants as are under the yoke count their own masters worthy of all honor." Now, the passage looks quite slavish. Why did not the apostle add, after the word "honor," "*for this is right?*" When he claims "honor" for parents, he said to the children, "*for this is right.*"

On the slaveholder's hypothesis one member of the sentence must be cut off—the motive part: "that the name of God and his doctrine be not blasphemed." Here is trouble at the outset. But, this is only the "beginning of sorrows." Where will he find "the wholesome words of our Lord Jesus Christ, and the doctrine which is according to godliness," to help him safely through with the argument? "The doctrine which is according to godliness" must inculcate the practice of love, mercy, justice, righteousness toward all men; these, with all other godlike qualities.

Will this "word" of our Lord help him: "Thou shalt love thy neighbor as thyself?" If slaves are bought and sold, worked without compensation, deprived of education, etc., because their masters love them, love them in any other sense than a man loves an ox, or an ass, or any other brute; when he sells it for gold, or pays gold for it; then may this be to him a "wholesome word." Did ever one man enslave another because he loved him as he loved himself? Did the system originate in love? Is it perpetual in love? Every candid slaveholder would say No! No! to these questions. Will the following words of our Lord Jesus Christ be wholesome: "Therefore, all things whatsoever ye would that men should do unto you, do ye even so unto them; for this is the law and the prophets?" The practical application to the case in hand would be for the master to treat his slave, precisely as he would wish to be treated, if himself were the slave. So I do, says the slaveholder. Grant it for the present. But, is there not a manifest fallacy here? This application of this "word" of our Lord does not reach far enough back. There was a time when the master was not the master, and when the slave was not the slave.

To deal honestly with this "wholesome word," it must be applied to the time when the master laid his hand upon his slave, and said, You are my property; and not the subsequent condition of his slave, who was once a man, but now, by an act of his master, converted into a chattel, and then say, If I were a chattel this treatment would be good enough for me. But who made this man a chattel?—a thing? If I were as degraded as he, I should neither expect nor deserve better treatment than I give him. If I were a slave, said a master, I would not be deserving of that respect due to a free man. I would only look for what is due to those of my rank. Ah! master, who made me a slave?

Every slave-code, ancient and modern, defines a slave to be a "thing"—not a man, but a "thing"—to be disposed of as other things. Slaveholders conceive of their slaves in the light of the statute book of the State, not in the light of the statute book of heaven. According to their ideas of a slave, that golden rule of right—"all things whatsoever ye would that men should do unto you, do ye even so to them"—does not at all apply to the rights of their slaves, as the implied obligations relate to men, not to things of merchandise.

Therefore, they never apply it in any question of duty to their slaves. It may be safely questioned, whether ever a slaveholder tried the rectitude of his doings toward his slaves, by this heart-searching, unerring rule of right, and continued to be a slaveholder. "Therefore, all things," etc. That these are some of the wholesome words of our Lord Jesus Christ, will be admitted by all. But they are not very wholesome to slaveholders, unless they can honestly say before God, that they "would that men should" enslave them and their wives and their children, and hold them in slavery, and treat them accordingly. But who would believe such a declaration? No sane man. Therefore, none but a fool or a hypocrite would make such a statement.

"For the laborer is worthy of his hire," Luke x: 7, is another wholesome word of our Lord Jesus Christ. On which side is this? On the side of freedom, or on the side of slavery? Slavery looks quite demurely at this, and says, by way of reply, "The laborer is not worthy of any hire; *therefore I give my laborers no 'hire.'*"

We now resign all that Jesus Christ said and commanded to the friends of slavery, and ask them kindly to bring forward one sentence from Matthew, Mark, Luke, or John, that would be favorable to the system. Nay, we challenge them to the effort. They will do it if they can. The present turn of the controversy requires this at their hands. Mind—the question now to be settled, is, on which side of the controversy were Paul's proud men, who would not "consent to the wholesome words of our Lord Jesus Christ?" That the teachings of our Lord are in favor of freedom, is not a debatable question. Freedom is one of the "things against which there is no law." But are his "words" also in favor of bondage? *This is the question.* The answer belongs to the affirmative.

But we must also examine the "doctrine" which grew out of the great commission—the "doctrine which is according to godliness." "Teaching them (the baptized) to observe all things whatsoever I have commanded you." We might assume, without fearing the charge of being too credulous, that this doctrine is on the side of freedom. Elder Franklin says "it is." "Hundreds of good men yielding to that preference which the Bible gives to freedom over slavery, in the emancipation of all the slaves that fell into their hands." This is good testimony coming from the other side of the house. Paul says, those who will not "consent" to these Bible "preferences for freedom" over slavery, are "proud men of corrupt minds"—as such they are to be "withdrawn from."

Well, "love worketh no ill to his neighbor." But "love" works something to his "neighbor." If not ill, then *good.* Yes, *good,* so all the world would decide. This doctrine suggests a question: is it a *good* or an *ill* to enslave a man, or to hold in slavery those who are enslaved by others? The direction of this "doctrine" is too obvious to justify even a comment. If all the moral principles and precepts found in the Epistles of the Apostles to the churches were collated, "Love worketh no ill to his neighbor—therefore love is the fulfilling of the law," would be but a descriptive caption to the entire list.

"For, if thou mayest be made free, use it rather." This is moderate abolitionism. If you may not be made free, make yourself free by emigration. This is radical abolitionism. The moderate and the radical agree in this, namely, that slaves should be liberated. They only differ as to the means. But Paul says, in the same connection, "Be not ye the servants (slaves) of men." No radical can be more radical than this.

"Of a truth I perceive that God is no respecter of persons." Why is only one race among the many doomed to slavery by the American people? Why do they make large contributions to educate the heathen in distant lands, and not only make no appropriations to educate some millions, who are home-born—who plow their fields—who reap their harvests—who sweep their houses—wash their clothes—cook their dinners—but have, by legislative enactments, made it a crime to be punished by law, to educate one of these native Americans? The answer is clearly this—they are respecters "of persons." Hence this ungodly partiality. The man that has one-half—one-fourth—one-eighth—one-sixteenth, or less of the blood of these despised "persons" in him, must be doomed to ignorance—systematically deprived of all and every branch of education—save only what will make him profitable to his owner, as an ox is broken to the yoke, or an ass to the harness. *Is this according to the "doctrine of godliness?"* When God set on foot a system of education—when he sent his Son into the world on this business, he opened the door to all; nay more, he sent the word of his salvation to all nations—*Ethiopia not excepted.* It was this impartiality that made an apostle exclaim, "Of a truth I perceive that God is no respecter of persons." "The doctrine which is according to godliness," must recognize this "truth" in all its practical phases—must recognize it as God recognized the equality of all nations in the mission of his Son, as developed by the wholesome words of our Lord Jesus Christ, and more fully elaborated by the apostle's preaching and teaching.

To advocate slavery is to advocate the doctrine of partialism in its widest extremes; a doctrine as unlike God as Christ is unlike Belial; differing from "the doctrine which is according to godliness," as the blackest of American "black laws" differ from the "wholesome words of our Lord Jesus Christ."

We shall next examine verse 2d: "And they that have believing masters," etc.

ESSAY VIII.

"AND they that have believing masters, let them not despise them, because they are brethren; but rather do them service, because they are faithful and beloved partakers of the benefit. These things teach and exhort." 1st Tim. vi: 2.

The advocates of slavery place more reliance upon the first four verses of this chapter, than all the New Testament beside. Whatever may be obscure in the sense of the 1st and 2d verses, must be made plain by the 3d verse. "If any man teach otherwise, and consent not to wholesome words, even the words of our Lord Jesus Christ, and the doctrine which is according to godliness," etc. This is the key. It is to the passage, including the first ten verses, what the key-note is in music. It must decide on which side of the question the teachers were, from which Timothy was to "withdraw himself." Teachers, who were teaching on the subject of slavery, a doctrine contrary to the doctrine of Christ, were to be the subjects of correction and discipline. This was the specific object of this part of the epistle. Slavery is in the passage *only* by implication. Some teachers were either ignorant or obstinate. They would not consent to the standard authority—to the teachings of Christ and his Apostles. But for these teachers who are complimented by the apostle with being both proud and ignorant, we should not have this item of instruction to Timothy, and through him to the churches; for the occasion which called it forth, would not have existed.

Now to the issue. Did Paul in his instructions to Timothy, as to the course he should pursue with these false teachers, justify slavery, as it then existed in the Roman empire? Here the teachers differ. Some say he did, others say he did not. Whatever he taught in this place, directly or indirectly, upon the practical aspects of the subject, must have been "according to the words of Jesus Christ and the doctrine of godliness." The teachings of those animadverted upon were the per contra. Paul and these teachers were belligerents. Timothy, as the superintendent of the church at Ephesus, was required to proceed against them. He was first to charge *them* to desist from "teaching another doctrine." See 1st Tim. i: 3. Then, if they still persisted, and would not "consent to the wholesome words of our Lord Jesus Christ and the doctrine which is according to godliness," he was required to *withdraw* from them. These teachers were *heretics*, (*schismatics*,) for they were "causing divisions and offenses contrary to the doctrine which they had learned." "A man that is a heretic, after the first and second admonition, reject." Titus iii: 10.

If our Lord and Savior Jesus Christ and his Apostles were *pro-slavery* preachers, these were *anti-slavery* preachers. And, *vice versa:* If Jesus Christ and the Apostles were *anti-slavery* preachers, these were *pro-slavery* preachers; for on the subject of slavery these parties taught contrary doctrines.

Pro-slavery pleaders assume that Christ and his Apostles were *pro-slavery* preachers. This is precisely what all errorists have and do assume, whether Papists or Protestants. Universalists claim, that the inspired preachers taught the doctrine of universal salvation; Calvinists claim that they preached the doctrine of unconditional election and reprobation; Pædo-Baptists that they taught the doctrine of infant sprinkling; and slaveholders, whether such in principle or practice, that they were the stanch advocates of the rightfulness of human slavery. Each, in his own way, appeals to the Bible for the defense of his own dogma. No doctrine or practice in professed christendom, however *monstrous* and *absurd*, but has looked to the Bible for justification. But all these, and other errorists, look to other sources for instruction. Universalists get their instruction from Winchester, Ballou, and some lesser lights; and then go to the Bible for the defense of that they never learned from its pages. Calvinists study Calvin's Institutes, and listen to some of his retailers for instruction in doctrine, and then appeal to the Word of Inspiration for defense of what they learned in other books—were taught by teachers *sent not* by God, but by men. Pro-slavery teachers, in the primitive church, took their lessons from the Roman Slave Code, based upon the antichristian *axiom*, that "*might* gives *right;*" and then sought to incorporate this cruel, bloody doctrine with the "Gospel of Peace," and universal "good will among men." In this they followed the judaizers and philosophers who, to some extent, succeeded in blending their corruptions with the "pure" and "holy" Gospel of Christ. But the Apostles, endued with a divine vigilance, descried these corrupters and warned the evangelists and elders against their innovations. Hence our text and its parallels: "If any man consent not to wholesome words," etc.

The pro-slavery teachers, with whom we are concerned, have received their instructions from *kidnappers*—from manstealers; from the national and State constitutions; local slave laws; fugitive slave bills; the decision of courts, and a corrupt public sentiment; and to these we may add the self-contradictory and suicidal teachings of some apologizing scribes, who say they are opposed to slavery, and in the same paragraph say, that "both Moses and Paul—Old and New Testaments—admit and sustain the relation of bond-servant and bond-master for life." From these sources they receive their instructions, and then go to the Bible for justification. They have made at least a show of defense; so have the advocates of popery and of prelacy. Can they make a better effort in defense of slavery by an appeal to the Bible, than baby sprinklers?

Many of the good, the pious, and the learned, practice infant baptism, and honestly believe it to be the baptism ordained by Jesus Christ and practiced by the

Apostles. Thousands have of late years been convinced that it was a mere show of defense; by twisting and bending the Scriptures to support a convenient, a favorite, a popular proselyting dogma. Begotten and born outside the Bible, and then brought to the Bible for confirmation, to be christened *Christian Baptism.*

There is no system of ecclesiastical or civil corruption and tyranny, that has not, by false issues and interpretations, claimed Bible justification and defense. In divers times and places, the divine right of kings is defended with as much argument and logic, as American slavery was or ever can be. There is no book on earth more liable to such "*wrestings,*" than the Bible. This was extensively done in the days of the Apostles; to which one of them is witness. "Wrest," the Epistles of Paul, "as they do also the other Scriptures, unto their own destruction." 2d Pet. iii: 16.

This liability to be wrested is unavoidable from its variety of subject and brevity in detail. Still, there is a spirit of purity, of righteousness, of benevolence, underlying the whole, which will ever be a safeguard to the "single-hearted."

The Bible will defend its own begotten children. It does this freely, voluntarily. It does this to the satisfaction of children, and the clearest apprehension of the upright in heart, to all who have no selfish object to subserve, when they open its inspired pages. But illegitimates it will not defend; though often forced upon it for support, it will not receive them. Though importuned by adulterous and interested fathers, it will reject them. It will, with the firmness of God, say they are not mine. It has always said, and it now says:

"the Papacy is not one of my children. Though she has promised the Bible great numbers and emoluments, but *the* book says, she is a whore in scarlet attire, and I will expose her; I will put her to shame."

All questions, which have to be forced upon the Bible, are foreign and extraneous subjects. When the subject requires much learning, much talent, and much special pleading, to gain for it Bible support, you may set it down as a settled fact that it is not a Bible subject.

It requires no special pleading, no tact in controversy to show, that the Gospel is the devoted friend of freedom. A controversy on this subject would be something new. Its motto is: "*Glory to God in the highest, on earth peace, good will among men.*" All men and all nations are equally involved in sin; equally embraced in the plan of redemption; equally honored with a tender of the gospel; equally eligible to honor and promotion in the kingdom of heaven. There are no preferences originating in a "respect of persons;" God's love for all, claims a corresponding love to all, from all its subjects. In brief, that peace and good will among men is the all-pervading spirit of the gospel. This spirit is underlying the work of the Father, of the Son, and of the Holy Spirit; and all the labors, sufferings, and teachings of the Apostles and Evangelists of Jesus Christ.

The advocates of slavery must take one of three positions: 1st, either that this is not true of the gospel; or 2d, that slavery is in harmony with this; or 3d, that this is true of the gospel, with a small exception, namely a few specific passages in the Epistles of Paul and Peter touching slavery.

They will not take the 1st; for then all men would call them infidels. They will not take the 2d, for then all men would laugh at their folly. They will then take the 3d. Let us now see how this will affect the Gospel as a consistent system, claiming a divine origin. The Gospel then teaches both "good will" and ill will "among men;" (for even slaveholders will not say that slavery originated in good will to the enslaved.) It teaches both freedom and slavery. The man that is not blinded by interest or prejudice, would stop and think before he would give to the glorious gospel of Christ such a mixed character, and involve its benignant author in such gross inconsistency.

It would be modest upon the part of these teachers to admit at least the possibility that they had mistaken the true meaning of some five or six short passages in the Epistles, rather than to make a mere fractional part conflict with the balance of the inspired volume. Inasmuch as they have gotten the origin of the system, and all the barbarous regulations by which the system is kept up, outside the Bible, and only ask the Bible to canonize it, such admission on their part would be quite *graceful.* We ask this for their sake, not for the sake of the controversy; for to us it appears a little too coercive to require *Heaven* to father, and the *Church* to nurse the child begotten by the Devil (pirates) and born by their accomplices (purchasers).

Some of the passages here alluded to, pressed into pro-slavery service, we have examined in former articles; but we shall look at them again, from another standpoint. If the teachers, from which Paul commanded Timothy to "*withdraw*" himself, preached anti-slavery doctrine, then Paul preached pro-slavery, and *vice versa*. Paul does not say affirmatively what they did teach on the subject of slavery, but negatively, that they would not "consent" to the "words" of Christ and the "doctrine" of "godliness;" and affirmatively, the effect of their teaching, namely that their preachings led "to envy, strife, railings, evil surmisings, perverse disputings of men of corrupt minds, and destitute of the truth, supposing that gain is godliness; from such withdraw thyself."

Might we not, without further investigation and fear of contradiction, claim that these teachers, now under the *ban* of excommunication, were the advocates of slavery, *outright human slavery?* "By their fruits you shall know teachers, though the wolf should seek to disguise himself under the fleece of a lamb."

The advocacy of freedom, of equal rights, of human rights, of love to all mankind, never produced the bitter fruits here enumerated. But, on the contrary, such are, and such ever have been, the legitimate fruits of slavery in the slaveholder's family; in the slave or negro quarters; in the field, in the church, in the State; and such must of necessity be the consequences of the system.

"Supposing that gain is godliness." Can this apply to the man who advocates the principles of universal freedom? Did those benevolent men, who advocated the abolition of West India slavery, do so for the sake of gain? What pecuniary advantage did they expect to reap as a reward for their toil? What selfish object has aroused so many in our own country to plead the cause of the oppressed? You may set aside all who have made it an infidel or political hobby, and then you have the true anti-slavery stamina left, who are preaching and praying for the abolition of American slavery, without the promise or hope of worldly "gain." Nay, the opposite is true in their case. "Supposing that gain is godliness" will not apply to anti-slavery pleaders. "From such withdraw thyself," could not have been from anti-slavery teachers. But is it not probable that it will apply to pro-slavery teachers? Slaveholders are the rich. To secure the favor of the rich is no mean item of gain. The rich are the honorable, the popular and the influential. To "gain" influence and power, is only to "gain" the favor of slaveholders. But again, to be a consistent slaveholder, and to enjoy all the gain arising from the system, a man must advocate the rightfulness of one man laboring, and another being the exclusive receiver of the benefit. And this is not all: he must also maintain, that it is just and right of one man to own another man; to own this other man's wife, and his children, in the same sense that he owns the horses in his stable, or the cooking utensils in his kitchen. Any system, profession, or business that creates wealth, gives ease, power, or influence, is "gain." Slavery proposes all these objects of human desire and pursuit to the masters, but places them out of the reach of the slave, and that *for ever*; but universal freedom proposes the equal distribution of these lawful objects of human industry and ambition, and upon an equal basis places them within the reach of all.

Therefore, those who plead the cause of emancipation from principle, influenced by no mixed motives, are beyond the reach of honorable suspicion—that they are actuated by objects of worldly "gain." Nay, the history of the past is a sufficient apology for the purity and disinterestedness of their motives. They have, without exception, lost *place*, *caste*, and *favor* with those in power: have been mobbed, tarred and feathered, whipped, imprisoned, lynched, and murdered; have been denounced as disturbers of the peace, agitators, fanatics, and men of one "idea;" modernism for *fool*. Who but an insane man would espouse and advocate such a cause with the hope of "gain?" But the other side of the question is full of hope, full of promise, especially so long as the slave power is moving all the wheels of society, in every department, as it always has in these United States, and did in the Roman empire, until the christian religion, by its godlike, benevolent spirit, in its youthful days, wrought out for it a most signal reverse.

"Supposing that gain is godliness." "Gain" in an ill sense, as the connection shows, was a feature in those teachers who would not "consent to the wholesome (healing) words of our Lord Jesus Christ." But there are yet other specifications in relation to those "teachers." "But they that will be rich," verse 9. This has a specific application in this connection. It is by every correct rule of interpretation applicable to those in the 5th verse, who supposed that "gain" was "godliness," and those in the 10th verse, who had "erred from the faith;" the same who in the 3d verse taught "otherwise" on the then "controverted question of slavery," than "the faith," or the gospel, and would "not consent to the wholesome words of Christ and the doctrine of godliness." In the 5th verse the apostle said to Timothy, "from such (teachers) withdraw thyself." Verse 11 changes the subject, and Timothy himself is the subject of address. "But thou, O man of God, flee these things;" the things taught by the teachers. Flee both the men and "the things." On whatever side of the question these teachers were, this is their *advertisement.*

1st, They would "not consent to the wholesome words of our Lord Jesus Christ, and the doctrine which is according to godliness."

2d, They supposed that "gain" was "godliness."

3d, They had "erred from the faith."

And 4th, The tendency of their teaching was "envy, strife, railings, evil surmisings," etc.

With this descriptive notice before us, we conclude that these teachers were on the affirmative of the question, and Paul on the negative, unless the 2d verse should lead to a different conclusion. "And they that have believing masters, let them not despise them, because they are brethren, but rather do them service, because they are faithful and beloved partakers of the benefit."

But for the designations "master" and "servant," no one would even suspect that the parties here referred to were master and slave. There is not a word here that looks like oppression. In the 1st verse, where the allusion is to unbelieving masters, it is quite otherwise. There we have the "yoke," "servants under the yoke." The word yoke here means slavery, and metaphorically, oppression. A deprivation of right is essential to slavery. Without this there is no slavery. As soon as a Roman master and his slave were *converted,* they stood in a new relation to each other: "*they are brethren.*" The duties of this new relation must so change and neutralize the prerogatives of the master over the slave, that the designation "*master*" can no longer be applied in its Roman or American sense.

"And they that have believing masters, let them not despise them." Suppose now the master continues to hold his slave, now a "brother," as he did when an unconverted heathen, can the servant obey this command? He can not help but "despise" him, the command to the contrary notwithstanding. God never made a man *mean* enough to honor such a master. But the master is his brother, therefore he must not despise him. For this reason he must despise him the more, if his master still holds him as a chattel, subject to the same legal and commercial vicissitudes as before their conversion. It would be a christian *virtue* to *despise* such a master; for what a man can approve in another, he can justify in himself. The enlightened christian slave, that could justify his professed christian master to continue the same course toward him as before their conversion, could justify himself in slaveholding, if he possessed the power.

A brother can only esteem a brother if he acts a brother's part. If not, the disesteem is in the proportion that one christian brother has a right to expect from another. Therefore, Paul did not command the servant *not* to despise his master because he was his master, but because he was his *brother*. It is worthy of remark here, that in all the instructions to servants, there is not one duty enjoined upon them toward their masters, because they are their masters. The duty to respect, to honor, or to obey, is always drawn from some other consideration. We shall give a few examples.

1st. "Servants be obedient to them that are your masters," etc., "in singleness of your heart as unto Christ." "Not with eye-service as men-pleasers, but as the servants of Christ, doing the will of God from the heart. With good will doing service, as to the Lord, and not to men." Eph. vi.

2d. "Servants obey," etc., "not with eye-service as men-pleasers, but in singleness of heart, fearing God. And whatsoever ye do, do it heartily, as unto the Lord and not unto men," etc., "for ye serve the Lord Christ." Col. iii.

3d. "That they may adorn the doctrine of God our Savior in all things." Titus ii: 10.

4th. "Servants, be subject to your masters," etc., "for this is thankworthy if a man for conscience toward God endure grief, suffering wrongfully." 1st Pet. ii: 18–19.

5th. Let as many servants as are under the yoke count their own masters worthy of all honor." (Why?) "That the name of God and his doctrine be not blasphemed." "And they that have believing masters, let them not despise them." (Why not?) "Because they are brethren."

These examples fully prove the position that the Apostles could find no motive to respect or obedience in the relation of master, or they would have enforced it. In other relations they found the motive to duty in the relation, and not in some remote consideration. To this we shall also cite a few examples: "Husbands love your wives." "The wife see that she reverence her husband." "Children obey your parents in the

Lord, for this is right." "Fathers, provoke not your children to wrath." "Love as brethren." "Honor all men." "Put them in mind to be subject to principalities and powers, to obey magistrates." "Submit yourself to every ordinance of man for the Lord's sake, whether it be to the king as supreme, or unto governors, as unto them that are sent by him." 1st Pet. ii: 13–14. "Let every soul be subject unto the higher powers. For there is no power but of God; the powers that be are ordained of God. Whosoever resisteth the power, resisteth the ordinance of God," etc. "Render therefore to all their dues; tribute to whom tribute is due, custom to whom custom, fear to whom fear, honor to whom honor."

In all these cases the duty to love, reverence, honor, obey, etc., grows out of the immediate relation, as things legitimate. But the relation of master is not even the proximate cause claiming obedience or honor from the servant. Here, then, is a marked difference between the slave relation and the other relations. This fact has placed a dark seal of reprobation upon this relation. The relation is recognized, but *not* respected. Its existence is admitted but *not* sustained. It is the subject of special legislation, but no duty is based upon it. Is the christian servant to honor his heathen master, *it is for the sake of the name of God and his word.* Is the believing servant to respect his believing master, *it is because they are brethren.* Let them not despise them because they are master and servant—*nay,* but because they are brethren. The old relation is named, but the duty to respect is based upon the new relation "because they are brethren." "But rather do them service because they are faithful."

"Faithful" as heathen masters? *Nay*, "faithful as brethren;" brethren in Christ, beloved by the servant, because the master is a "faithful" brother in the Lord—"partakers of the benefit." "*Parteneres of the benefice.*" (Tindal's translation.)

Neither of these readings will apply to slavery. There is no appreciable sense, in which the master and the slave can be said to be partakers in any thing touching the product of the slave's labor. It will not do to say that the slave lived upon the product of his own labor. This might be affirmed of a horse or a mule, in the same sense; for neither live for themselves. Their lives are valuable to another. Are they well fed and strong, it is to the interest of the owner, as physical debility would be no loss to them. The masters were partakers of the benefit. They were sharers or partners with their servants. The idea conveyed is mutual interest, a thing irreconcilable with slavery, but most reconcilable with christian brotherhood. But for the *noun* (master) the reader would not suspect that this passage had even the remotest allusion to slaves, as it is more descriptive of another relation, namely that of *Landlord* and *Tenant*. The tenant is a mere occupant of that which belongs to another; therefore he is the dependent, and may with great propriety be exhorted not to despise his more affluent brother, though more fortunate in worldly circumstances; he is nevertheless faithful to his poorer brother, and should be beloved by him. In this relation there is a reciprocity of interest corresponding to the text—"partakers" (parteneres) "of the benefit;" language wholly irreconcilable with slavery. And to urge this upon a slave as a motive to fidelity would be to add insult to injury.

Whatever Paul and Peter *did* mean by the designations "master" and "servant," when writing to christians, they *did* not use them in their current political import. In the State, the right of ownership, and therefore the duty to serve, are based directly upon the relation; in the New Testament *never*. The duties enjoined are subversive of the relation, because in harmony with the law of brotherly love. The titles Master and Servant, in their political value, can not be reconciled with christian relations, rights, and duties. Here is an impassable gulf. But it may be asked, why use them? It may not be so easy to give a satisfactory answer to this question. Still the fact can not be denied, that in the apostolic writings they do not express the rights and responsibilities they so clearly express in slave-codes, whether ancient or modern. If there is a difficulty here, the slaveholder has the harder side. Hard as it may be to reconcile the titles in their state import, with the duties as specified by Paul and Peter, he is nevertheless obliged to do it or give up his claim to the New Testament writers as pro-slavery preachers. But should we fail to solve this difficulty, we fail on mercy's side. But to the task:

1st. The parties were properly described by these titles before they were converted to christianity.

2d. They were still master and servant when converted.

3d. Whatever changes in this relation and duties to each other, were subsequent to their conversion to Jesus Christ.

4th. The change was not an instantaneous, but a gradual work, effected by the leavening process of the Gospel, as suggested to the parties by new and holy relations, new duties growing out of divine relations, and enforced by new motives—motives quickened into action by a new spirit, the spirit of God: therefore the same titles were appropriately applied to those in this relation, subsequent to their embracing the Gospel, and no abuse of language, or of principle, to continue the old titles so long as the parties continue together, though their relative position was so materially changed, as to be partakers in what they jointly produced by the capital of the one and the labor of the other.

This was giving to the servant what was just and equal. This was consenting to the "wholesome words of our Lord Jesus Christ." This was saying with him that "*the laborer is worthy of his hire.*" This, too, was "according to the doctrine of godliness;" namely "*that no man go beyond and defraud his brother in any matter.*" To require for servants what was "just and equal," could not fail to be offensive to those teachers who were opposed to Christ and his Apostles. They supposed that "gain" was "godliness," and slavery was "gain." To give servants what was "just and equal," to let them be "partakers" with their masters in the "benefit," was destroying the "gain" of the business. These teachers had long enjoyed the "gain" of oppression, and they were unwilling to give it up. Therefore Paul said: "Timothy, do you 'withdraw' from them."

The 2d verse teaches nothing peculiar, nothing different from the general instructions given to all christians:

1st, That christian brethren should not despise one another.

2d, That they should be faithful to one another.

3d, That they should love one another.

4th, That they should be partakers in whatever benefit might result from capital invested or labor performed. This is Paul's instruction to christian masters and servants. These instructions obeyed, must put an end to slavery and every form of unrighteous "gain."

We shall in our next look at the subject from a pro-slavery standpoint, with some remarks on Philemon.

ESSAY IX.

We have now, in several articles, examined the few passages in the Epistles which treat of slavery—the relation of master and servant, their duties, and the basis of the duties enjoined. To us it is quite certain that these teachings are *anti-slavery* in *sentiment*, and *abolishing* in *tendency;* as truly so, as were the instructions of the same Apostles to the churches opposed to Polygamy, the exposing of infants, and the abolition of those time-honored and law-established usages. These could once claim as much legal sanction and popular favor, as *human slavery*. They were indeed elements of the same order of society, and brought under the same corrective treatment by the gospel.

But, we have examined the subject with strong anti-slavery prepossessions, and we are fully conscious that a strong mental bias is not most favorable to a fair, impartial hearing of testimony. The mind may become as much enslaved as the appetite—may be as *servile* as the hand. Knowing this blinding, bewildering liability, in our weak, common humanity, we have resolved to look at the subject with the "mental bias" of a slaveholder. And this will we do without respect to results. No matter, now, how the conclusions may affect master or servant, Christ or the Apostles, the Gospel, the Church, or the State.

We have no superstitious reverence for the Bible. We are not responsible for its teachings on any subject, but we may be, and should be for the state of mind in which we allow ourselves to listen to its testimonies.

"With the pure thou wilt show thyself pure, and with the froward thou wilt show thyself froward." Ps. xviii: 26. In this we have the reason, why "many are *ever* learning, and *never* coming to the knowledge of the truth."

The man that asks God to justify his selfish, wicked schemes, is a "mocker," and should be left to "eat the fruit of his own doings."

In my present imaginary position, I find it most difficult to approach the subject without suspecting my motives. My exemption from manual labor, the love of ease, so dear to myself and family—my property, that for which I have paid a money consideration—are all involved in the conclusions to which this investigation shall conduct me. Try as I may, I fear there are still some mixed motives in my heart. A desire that my conclusions from inspired premises shall justify my position as a slaveholder, may "serve as a gift that blindeth the eye." But, to be as disinterested as possible, we shall imagine we are living in the city of Corinth, A. D. 59,—members of the church of Christ, founded by the Apostle Paul in A. D. 54, and some of us are *slaves.* The church is desirous for apostolic instruction on several questions, among the rest, that of slavery. A letter of inquiry is sent to the apostle; it has come to hand by return of our faithful messenger. The officiating elder to-day (Lord's Day), is now reading the epistle to the congregation—has just come to the seventh chapter—"Now concerning the things whereof ye wrote unto me," etc. "Art thou called, being a servant care not for it." I sympathise with you, "for, if thou mayest be made free, use it rather." You desire to be "free." You do not sin by indulging this desire; you should be "free," and if you can be "made free," use your opportunity. That these reflections are suggested by the text, I am compelled to admit; also, that this address to my servant implies that I should grant him his desire, and let him go "free."

Men have been suspected for being abolitionists, for saying *even* less than this. To encourage slaves in a desire for freedom—to hint to masters in terms however modest, that they should "free" their slaves, in the hearing of their slaves, would render a man obnoxious to the slave-power. It would be a violation of every slave-code, then, as well as now; and that the penalty would now be inflicted upon such offender, is as certain as life and death. If Paul would now say in Kentucky, what he said to the servants in the church at Corinth, he would be regarded as an abolitionist, and dealt with accordingly; unless his apostleship should save him from popular outrage, and penal stripes.

Imagining myself to be a slaveholder, I would be compelled, from the plain, obvious meaning of words, so to understand, and so to decide—namely, that this address to the slave members of the church, was directly calculated to make them more dissatisfied with the yoke.

Now, we will go to Ephesus, and hear Paul again on the same subject. "And ye, masters, do the same things unto them, forbearing threatening; knowing that ye also have a Master in heaven; neither is there respect of persons with him."—Eph. vi: 9. This epistle was publicly read in the congregation to masters and servants. The servants heard this injunction read to their masters—"*forbearing threatening*," and enforced upon them by the consideration, "you have a Master in heaven,"—a Master who respects the person of the "master," no more than the person of the slave. How would we slaveholders receive this address? Would we not fear the influence it might have upon our slaves? What! say to us in their presence, that we must quit "*threatening*" them with corporal punishment? How can we keep them in subjection only through fear? Let the apprehension of punishment be removed, and how long will they obey us? But, again, look at this: this Paul said to our slaves, that in the sight of God we are no better than they. Will not this make them proud? Will they not begin to think that they are about as good as we are, and claim equality with us, and therefore more liberty? He said, too, that we had a "Master in heaven." Will they not understand this to be a word of caution to us masters, to take care how we shall treat them? that our Master in heaven will hold us responsible?

If Paul had said all this to us privately: but, these slaves are ever ready to seize upon every thing that favor the idea of their being free, and this will make them think more highly of themselves, etc., etc.

Let this passage be stripped of its apostolic garb. Let its sacredness be laid aside. Let a stanger from the *North* use it as his own, when addressing slaveholders in the presence of their slaves, and will they not feel and speak as above described? Will not the speaker be called an *abolitionist?* intending to stir up a feeling of insubordination on the part of the slaves. The language is not pro-slavery, but anti-slavery—the sentiments inculcated are anti-slavery, and the man that would so speak to American slaveholders on slave territory, would expect to be *lynched*, or hope to escape on the credit of Paul—a thing quite problematical.

Now we will follow Paul to Colosse, and hear what he has to say to masters in that church.

"Masters, give to your servants that which is just and equal; knowing, that ye also have a Master in heaven." What is the plain, obvious meaning of this address to masters, and to myself in particular? How would I understand it, coming from one claiming no inspiration? supposing the command, "Masters, give unto your servants," etc., is enjoined now for the first time. That we may the better understand it, let us separate from it its antiquity and apostolic authority, and look at its bare, naked import. This is something new, would be the first impression. Does this demand in behalf of my servants call for more than the established usages in their case; i. e., food, raiment, shelter, and medicine when sick. This I have always given my servants. If no more than this, why this new requisition? If this new lawgiver, by the words "just and equal," claims more than the law which custom has ordained, as it would appear, then the question comes up, how much more? This dictator has not defined how much more. He has made the demand, and then says to me, "you have a Master in heaven;" "just and equal," as approved by "*your Master in heaven;*" "just and equal," according to the *balances of the sanctuary*.

If now, I shall acknowledge this new command as obligatory, here is my *strait*—how can I hold my servants as "things," and give them what is "just and equal" as men? No art, no sophistry, no play upon language, can help me out of my difficulty. I must either rebel against this new requisition made at my hands as a master, or give up my position as a slaveholder. To test the correctness of this reasoning, suppose some worthy gentleman, say in Virginia—one who had not been suspected for any anti-slavery leanings—should spring this doctrine upon that community, and advocate it with pen and tongue, in public and private, in the presence of masters and slaves—should enforce it upon Virginia slaveholders, that they should give their servants what was "just and equal," and apply the same motive to obedience, "You have a Master in heaven," all as his own view of what is right and dutiful—would he, in the Old Dominion, be considered orthodox or heterodox?—pro-slavery or anti-slavery? Reader, what is your answer? If this teaching would be opposed to slavery in Virginia, it was in Colosse. What it would be now, it was then. What the language would import, though not inspired, it would mean when clothed with apostolic authority—the only difference being, in the latter case it is decisive. I look at it now as a divine law—the word of God to me in relation to a grave, weighty question, a question involving my prerogatives as a master—constituted a master by an oppressive heathen government; but now by the grace of God I am a christian, and some of my servants by the same grace bestowed upon them are christians too. I must deal honestly with myself in this, as in all other questions of personal rights and relative duties. Being in possession of all the apostolic writings, a full and complete copy of the constitution and laws of the kingdom of heaven, I will take the laws upon this specific subject as a whole, as upon other specific questions, and then draw my conclusions. Not what is said to the Corinthians alone, to the Colossians alone, or to Philemon alone, but what in view of all the divine teachings upon the subject. This course will be candid—then may I say, "Lord, I have heard thy testimonies." This premised, I open the Book. The first thing, directly upon the subject of my present inquiry, is to servants—to my servants—"if thou mayest be made free, use it rather." Here it is taken for granted, that my servants desire freedom; but, whether this desire, admitted to be lawful, can be gratified, is yet quite hypothetical. Why so? The will of the master may contravene. What now? A will to be "free," and a will to hold in bondage; opposing wills—conflicting wills between christian brethren, are they both holy? Are they both right? This question is suggested to the master—to myself. Now I must take an exception to this law, which has decided the desire for freedom to be lawful. This I can not do, for the law is from heaven; or, I must reconcile the conflicting interests between slavery and freedom, so that no injustice shall be done to my servants, and we live together on terms of christian peace and brotherly love. Could the master do this? *Never* could he extinguish in the heart of an enlightened christian slave, the *love of freedom*—a desire declared to be lawful by the highest authority under heaven, by the Word of God. This would have been the more embarrassing, when we consider that the slaves in the days of the Apostles were white slaves—a people once as free and honorable as their masters—differing only, as the present nations of Europe, as the English and Scotch now differ in their customs and manners.

The master could not have recourse to violence, for the law says, Masters, "*forbear threatening*," for you have a "*Master in heaven.*" What then? *Emancipation* or *compromise?* How compromise? Who shall settle the terms? The parties? *No.* Slaves have no right to negotiate on any subject. True, it is so in the State; but the parties have become members of the church, and have come under its jurisdiction. The obligations of the last associations into which men enter, are always most binding. And when former obligations conflict, they must either be set aside, or so modified as to harmonize with the more recent responsibilities. The parties in question, as soon as one or both became subject to the law of Christ, incurred new responsibilities on all questions of morality and religion. Therefore, whatever in the past was incoherent with the present, had to be subject to correction. This is so when men enter into any new social compacts, In this fact, we find all that is profitable in passing from one social state to another. Aside from this, there can be no rational motive for change, as a change of organization would propose no object of advantage. Upon this universally admitted fact, that the last system of government, law, rule, or order, a man adopts, must have the precedence, the Apostles based their right of interference with the former doings and behavior of the members of the church. "That ye put off concerning the former conversation, the old man, which is corrupt according to the deceitful lusts, and be renewed in the spirit of your mind: and that ye put on the new man, which after God, is created in righteousness and true holiness."—Eph. iv: 22, 23, 24. This right of interference, every master and every slave conceded when he entered the kingdom of heaven. By this concession, they voluntarily came under apostolic jurisdiction; therefore, Paul could, without arrogance or stretch of authority, espouse the cause of the oppressed and remove the yoke, or, so modify it as not to conflict with the rights and duties of the "new man," "created in righteousness and true holiness." Hence, Paul, let it be borne in mind, decided first of all that servants were entitled to freedom, if thou mayest be made free," etc.; if not freedom, then, what is "just and equal." "*Justice* and *equality*" between man and man, and there *never would have been a slave*—there never would have been such an anomaly in the world as a *man thing*. Justice and equality will undo what injustice and inequality have done; therefore the philosophy of the command, "Masters, give unto your servants what is just and equal," as neither less nor more could be required, "according to the doctrine of godliness." This done, and the master and servant are "*partakers of the benefit*," and the relations and duties are so modified, as to make them consistent with the morality of the gospel. Such would be my understanding of the divine teachings upon this subject, my bias to the contrary notwithstanding.

But there is yet another feature in this subject, claiming grave consideration at the hand of every master, viz.: *what is the duty of believing masters toward their unbelieving servants?* Upon this we have no direct instruction; but we have that which is quite suggestive. "If believing servants were required to count their unbelieving masters worthy of all honor, that the name of God and his doctrine would not be blasphemed" by them, but that their christian deportment toward their masters would have a favorable, winning and converting influence, upon their masters, what would this suggest to a believing master with reference to his unbelieving slaves? The enlightened christian master, knowing that "God is no respecter of persons," that the souls of his slaves are as precious in the sight of the Lord as his own; that the same provision was made for them in the redemption which is by Jesus Christ—would naturally be led to inquire, will the just and merciful God require less of the believing master than of the believing servant? Less, than to pursue such a course toward his unbelieving slaves, that that which will win them to Christ, that they may enjoy "salvation with eternal glory." This inference flowing so legitimately from the premises, should bow the spirit of a slaveholder before God. It should come to him like thunder tones. It should rest upon his heart like a fiery law issuing from Mount Calvary—from him who died for slaves as well as for masters, and make them ask, "Lord, what wilt thou have me to do" in this case? I confess that I have bought these men as though they were beasts; they know I have the power to sell them as beasts. I have robbed them of all the rights and honors of humanity. I have degraded them in this, that I have chattelized them. What shall I do? Respect them as men, treat them as men, "that the name of God and his doctrine be not blasphemed" by them on your account. Make them feel and know that they are men; that they have souls to be saved, or to be lost. By your godly deportment, win them to the gospel of Christ. Can I do this, and maintain my present position toward them? What a question? *Who is sufficient for the answer?* God forbid that I should ever incur such a responsibility. But had I really incurred this responsibility in the days of my ignorance, I would seek by all lawful, by all possible means to be released from it. The man that fears God will not jeopardize his own salvation nor yet the salvation of others.

We can readily conceive how a christian slave could exert a saving influence upon an unbelieving master; but how a christian master could exert a saving influence upon an unbelieving slave, and treat him as a slave, is a problem I presume not to solve. But, it may be said, there are many masters whose slaves are members with them in the same church. To this we answer, there are masters who are better than the system, as there are infidels who are vastly better men than any system of infidelity could make them. There are masters whose bearing toward their slaves is rather that of parents toward minor children, than that of slaveholders. That such masters would exert a saving influence over their slaves is quite presumable. It is the legal prerogative for the master to sell his slaves, when his interest or necessity should demand, to whom he pleases, to be taken to any slave territory the purchaser may prefer. But there are a few of the many masters who will not sell a slave under any circumstances, and there are a few more who will only sell insubordinate slaves, to get rid of a pest, and punish *crime*. Property-crime! How strange! There are parents whose influence upon their children is damning. Their children know them to be hypocrites, and yet they are members with them in the same church. The influence of such parents is negative, but another influence may be positive, and decide the sons and daughters for Christ. So in this case.

But we are sure that the slaveholder who acts the part of the slaveholder, can exercise no saving power over his slaves, be his professions what they may. The slave will say, and should say, if my master is a christian, *I don't want to be a christian.* If he has religion, *I don't want religion*—and all the people should say, *Amen and amen.*

ESSAY X.

THE last thing to notice upon this subject, is Paul to Philemon. "I beseech thee for my son Onesimus, whom I have begotten in my bonds; which in time past was to thee unprofitable, but now profitable to thee and to me; whom I have sent again: thou therefore receive him, that is mine own bowels; whom I would have retained with me, that in thy stead he might have ministered to me in the bonds of the gospel. But without thy mind would I do nothing, that thy benefit should not be as it were of necessity, but willingly. For perhaps he therefore departed for a season, that thou shouldest receive him for ever. Not now as a servant but above a servant—a brother beloved, especially to me, but how much more unto thee both in the flesh and in the Lord. If thou count me, therefore, as a partner, receive him as myself. If he hath wronged thee, or oweth thee aught, put that to mine account," etc.

Our opponents assume that Onesimus was Philemon's slave. This was probably, but *not certainly* so. No sober man would feel safe to rest very important issues upon such evidence. They assume again, that Onesimus ran away from his master Philemon. Perhaps so; but Paul don't say so. He says he "departed." He may have "departed" with the consent of his master; as fathers sometimes consent to the departure of minor sons, because they are discontented and unprofitable at home. There is, indeed, so much of the hypothetical in their argument drawn from this epistle, that unless they are permitted to assume much and affirm more, they can not *even* make a show of defense.

It is hardly reconcilable with a high moral conscientiousness, to seize upon a passage as indefinite as this, and make it subserve a cause so grave, so weighty as American slavery. As a Jew said, in answer to Monsieur Voltaire—"the weightier the calumny, the clearer should be the proof of it." The evidence upon which a good man, a disinterested man, would base the defense of a system so serious in its bearings upon the social conditions of human society—a system invading all the natural rights of so many, with all the certain and solemn bearings of the eternal future—would require the testimony to be as clear, as transparent, as conclusive, as the testimony that Jesus of Nazareth arose from the dead. We could not suspect a man's motive, who was advocating upon inconclusive evidence that which was beneficent, just, and equal, while it would be quite otherwise with the man who would in any way aid or abet that which had a direct tendency to promote inequality among men, and increase the sum total of human wretchedness and wo.

But, grant the slaveholders' assumption that Onesimus was a fugitive slave when Paul found him in Rome. This admitted for the sake of the argument, and we concede nothing to the credit of slavery. Slaves escaped from their masters in the first century, as they do in the nineteeth century. If the running away of Onesimus had been a rare case, it would not reflect upon the system; but when running away from masters is a thing so common, as it always was, and now is, the fact would naturally prompt the inquiry, why is it so? How few ever become fugitives from other relations. *Fugitive husbands, fugitive wives, fugitive sons, fugitive daughters*—cases of this kind have not been frequent enough to originate the terms. But, *fugitive slave* is language as common and familiar as household words. The fugitives from all other relations would not support an "underground *hack*," while the fugitives from slavery furnish ample business for many "underground railroads." This fact tells its own story. It declares in the most unmistakable language that there is something in the relation most afflictive; therefore, the general discontentment of slaves, and the exceedingly hazardous experiment of running away from their oppressors. The legal guaranties to masters to recapture their fugitives, and all the aids they may press into their service, are but so many confirmations of the same fact. Why no legal arrangements for husbands to recapture their fugitive wives, and parents to bring back by the strong arm of statute law their runaway children. Why no *Fugitive Wife bill? Fugitive Children bill*, and marshals to execute them?

Onesimus being discontented and unhappy, sought to better his circumstances by running away from his master. He preferred to be a fugitive in a hostile world, rather than to be a slave at home. In this condition Paul found him, converted him, and sent him back to Philemon: "Whom I have sent again, thou therefore receive him, that is my own bowels,"—("own heart," German translation,)—"sent again." All that Paul could have meant by "*sent again*," was, that he made the proposition to Onesimus to return, and Onesimus consented to do so. *His return was voluntary.* If Paul had coerced him back, the case would present a different aspect. Onesimus was now in fact, if not in form, free, and that freedom he might have maintained by continuing in Rome. That he had something to say, and suggest, in regard to his future condition, in case he should return, is even more than probable. In whatever condition, he was to return to Philemon in that state, Philemon was to receive him. Now, what does the epistle, of which Onesimus was the bearer, say on this point? "For perhaps he departed for a season, that thou mightest receive him for ever; not now as a servant, but above a servant, a brother beloved." If Philemon refused to "receive" him as "a brother beloved," Onesimus was under *no* obligation to remain with him. Every hint and suggestion is in perfect harmony with this view of the case. Onesimus is "my son," and your "brother." "Receive him, that is mine own bowels." "If thou count me therefore a partner, receive him as myself;" "Receive him for ever." Philemon could not have received Onesimus as a servant, unless he would have received Paul as a servant. And in *no sense* could he have received him "*for ever*," as a servant, but he could have received him for ever as a "*brother beloved*." "Whom I would have retained with me that in thy stead he might have ministered unto me in the bonds of the gospel." For Paul to have retained Onesimus, would have been doing no injustice to Philemon, or Paul would not have thought of doing so. Had Paul done this, he would have set Onesimus free from his master; as Onesimus could not have ministered to Paul at Rome, and to Philemon at Colosse. In that case, the "*benefit*," which from the connection could be nothing else than *freedom*, would have been from "necessity" on the part of Philemon. But the apostle desired the "benefit" to be bestowed upon Onesimus, to be Philemon's free and voluntary act. "But, without thy mind I would do nothing, that thy benefit should not be as it were of necessity, but willingly." This was a delicate *touch*, but a *plain* hint. "That thy benefit,"—this was something to be conferred upon Onesimus. What could this "benefit" have been, if it was not freedom?

It could not have been to receive him as a brother, for that was strictly enjoined upon Philemon. It could not have been kind treatment, for, so good a man as Philemon would need no hint to that effect. It must have been something more than was due to a slave as such—more than the system of slavery required at the hand of masters; something befitting new and honorable relations—a "benefit" worthy of Paul's "son," and worthy of Philemon, "brother beloved" in the Lord. What this could have been short of manumission, we could not conjecture. This would have been in harmony with the spirit of the letter, and the kind of reception Paul bespoke for his son Onesimus. Then the apostle closed this part of the epistle with this comprehensive sentence. "Having confidence in thy obedience, I wrote unto thee knowing that thou wilt also do more than I say." "Having confidence in thy obedience." He commanded Philemon, upon the most endearing considerations, to receive Onesimus, "Not *now* as a servant,"—this is a negative command. If Philemon received Onesimus as a servant, he disobeyed the command; but if he received him as "above a servant, a brother beloved," he did what was enjoined upon him. To receive a man as a "brother beloved," *is to receive him in the highest and most honorable sense imaginable.* More can not be asked in behalf of any brother, unless it were a slave brother. To ask more in this case, would be *manumission.* This, Paul did not say, or command Philemon, but called his attention to it by a modest suggestion—"That thy benefit should not be as it were of necessity, but willingly." Now Philemon, I have confidence in you that you will do all for Onesimus, your brother, I have commanded you, "thou wilt also do more than I say."

We are the more confirmed in the correctness of this view, when we consider that Paul would not have conceded *less* to Onesimus, as a question of right, than *freedom*. "If thou mayest be made free, use it rather," would apply to Onesimus with as much force as to the servants in the church in Corinth. Therefore, Paul could, with great propriety, enjoin upon Philemon, as he did enjoin upon other masters, duties which would neutralize the relation between him and Onesimus, leaving him free to carry out his suggestion to liberate him, or to hold him still a slave. Let Philemon himself decide the question, whether he could receive Onesimus as he would have received Paul in his own person —receive him with the same affection and tenderness Paul expressed for Onesimus his son, "begotten in the bonds of the gospel;" "receive him not now as a servant, but above a servant, a brother beloved," and treat him accordingly, and yet continue to hold him in the degraded condition of a slave. Philemon would readily see his *strait*. If he did the latter, he could not do the former as commanded; to do the former, he must bestow the "*benefit*."

This epistle is of inexpressible value in the present controversy. Here the relation of master and servant, and that of brethren in Christ, with their claims and conflicts, are made to appear in all their entangling influences. These relations are antipodes; they are perfect antagonisms. Can these warring relations exist together in active, healthful exercise, so that each relation shall secure to the subjects of it, all that is contemplated in the relation? As much depends upon formal statement, we will state the question thus: could Philemon, as master, reap the full benefit of slavery from the person of Onesimus, his slave, and Onesimus, as slave, enjoy the full benefit of christian brotherhood from the person of Philemon, his master? If Philemon could exercise all the prerogatives of master, as defined by Roman or American slave-codes, and deprive Onesimus of education; inflict upon him corporal punishment according to the canons of the system, and sell him to the highest bidder as interest or inclination might dictate, without violating the law of brotherly love as taught in the gospel, or damage to his brother Onesimus, then may these relations exist together, operate together, and secure to the master and the slave all the advantages—all the good proposed by slavery on the one hand, and christianity on the other.

But, the reader will say, Philemon could not exercise these prerogatives, and honor and maintain his profession as a christian. Then, as soon as Philemon became a christian, he *ceased* to be a master in *fact*. This would be true of other relations.

When a husband can no longer claim "reverence" from his wife, as her matrimonial head, he ceases to be a husband. When parents are proscribed in their natural and legal rights, when they may no longer claim filial respect and obedience from their minor children, the relation is dissolved in all its practical phases. And, if the profession of christianity contravenes the *State* rights of the master, he is no longer a master in the practical import of that designation. To suppose that the religion of Jesus Christ did not interfere with the State rights of Roman masters—that it does not now conflict with the legal rights of American masters, is but a *poor* compliment to our wise and benevolent Redeemer.

An effort to harmonize the relation of master and slave with the relations of christianity, is the *rudest assault* ever committed upon the gospel of peace. An attempt (for that is all that ever was or can be done) to reconcile relations originating in *war* and *piracy*, with relations originating in infinite mercy and benevolence, betrays great ignorance or desperate wickedness. There is eternal enmity between these relations and their respective rights and duties. Such is their hostility, that they can never live in peace in the same house, be members of the same family. They are like the two forces in the physical world, one repelling and the other attracting. The one separated Philemon and Onesimus, both good men, for they proved themselves to be such. It was not their fault, but the fault of the system.

Onesimus would rather quit his slave home, and be a homeless, houseless, wandering fugitive, than be the slave of Philemon. And what Onesimus did, has been done a thousand times—*ten thousand times* told. How strong the repelling power!! But, the gospel, with its attractive influences, brought Onesimus back to his forsaken, deserted home. Ah, yes, Philemon is a christian now, and Onesimus has just become a christian. Now, Paul said to Onesimus—my son, will you go back to Philemon? Philemon, too, is my son; and, therefore, he is your brother. He owes me infinitely more than you owe him. I will not exact upon him, and he will not upon you. You left him a slave, now go back a "brother beloved," and you will be received as such. Onesimus—I will go back. Paul—Well, peace be with you; here is an epistle to your brother Philemon, etc. The relations leading to such different results, must be opposites. What, under heaven, so repulsive to our social feelings as slavery? And what so inviting, so attractive to man's social *nature*, as christianity, with its endearing relations of brother, sister, etc.?

In all the divine teachings, the rights and duties of these relations have the precedence. The rights of former relations conflicting with these, had to be given up, and personal responsibility was placed upon a new basis; "old things passed away, and behold all things became new." The new man, in his new relations to Christ, is a new "creature;" in all his doings, he is governed by new motives. His own spiritual and eternal interest, and that of others, must have the ascendency. "Seek first the kingdom of God and his righteousness." "Look not every man upon his own things only, but also upon the things of others," is a law of the kingdom of heaven, binding upon all its subjects. This law alone, in its practical tendency, would abolish the relation of master and slave. The relation of master is that of secular gain. It is the essence of the most supreme selfishness. His attachments to his slaves may be as strong as that of a covetous man to his gold, and similar in kind. *A money interest is the only bond between the master and his slaves.* Money considerations are creating and dissolving the relation, and that continually—*daily*. This is the lawful—legitimate—and necessary fruit of the system. Slaves are as much the staple, in some slaveholding States, as wheat is the staple production of Iowa. They have slave markets, and we have wheat markets. Slaves are their source of wealth, and wheat is ours. If there were no market for surplus slaves, there would be no motive to breed them; and if there were no market for our surplus wheat, wheat raising would cease to be business.

In Jesus Christ, selfishness must yield to christian sympathy; unrighteousness must yield to righteousness. There is no fellowship between these. One or the other must have the ascendancy. If slavery has the ascendancy, christianity has not. If christianity has, slavery has not. Slavery and christianity are not homogeneous. They have no affinity for each other. Slavery is older than christianity. Slavery had taken possession when Jesus Christ sent forth his Apostles to preach to the nations. If slavery had been an approved element of society, its right of occupancy would not have been disputed by them. They would have taken it as it was, and would have treated it with respect, as they did civil government, and other relations of society. They would have acknowledged the rightfulness of the relation, and would have enforced the current duties, as then established by the usages of society. They would have given permanence to the institution with a view to its continuance in the church. They would have made no concessions to slaves, or have enforced no duties upon masters. They would not only have taken it into the church as it was, but would have let it remain as they received it. That they would have pursued this course upon the aforesaid supposition, all will admit. Did they? They did not.

The first thing directly upon this subject is a concession to servants. "Art thou called, being a servant, care not for it, for if thou mayest be made free, use it rather." This is an unequivocal admission to servants, that they have a right to freedom. The abettors of slavery have never conceded this to slaves as a matter of right. Indeed, they can not, without committing themselves to the implied duty. To withhold conceded right is fraud—so understood by all men. To acknowledge the rights of others, is, in all candor and straightforwardness, regarded as a pledge to sustain them in their admitted rights. Therefore, slaveholders pursue the safer policy, and deny to their slaves the right of freedom. And the poor, pitiful apologists have to do the same perhaps, not willingly, but for the sake of self-defense. They see the dilemma. For, if they say, with Paul, slaves are entitled to freedom, to be consistent, they must use all lawful means to make them "free." If they do this they are not the slaveholder's friends. Then their commercial, political, and religious communions with slaveholders, would all be broken up. Alas! alas! who can make such a sacrifice?

The last upon this subject is Paul to Philemon, concerning his servant Onesimus. This is a practical comment upon the first;—the concession to servants—"*if thou mayest be made free*," etc. Onesimus had given evidence that he desired freedom rather than slavery. His conversion could not extinguish this desire. His willing return to Philemon was not to enter slavery again, but, to be reconciled to his brother Philemon. If Paul had advised Onesimus to return to Philemon as a slave, it is not even presumable that he would have returned *at all*. And if Paul had sent him back for that object, he would have said so; but he said just the *contrary*. "Whom I have sent again," verse 12. "Not *now* as servant," verse 16. This view reconciles an apparent contradiction in this epistle to Philemon. That Onesimus was the slave of Philemon, is a legitimate inference; that he was not, is just as legitimate upon the slaveholders' hypothesis; namely, that Philemon was to receive Onesimus as he left him. That he left him a slave, and he should receive him again as a slave. How can this be? Can a slave as such be a debtor? Slaves are not known as contracting parties. Paul says to Philemon, "If he, (Onesimus,) hath wronged thee, or oweth thee aught, put that to mine account." Now, how could Onesimus have been a slave, and at the same time a debtor to Philemon, or any body else? Paul does not say that Onesimus had wronged Philemon, or that he owed him any thing. The language is hypothetical—"If he oweth thee aught." The apostle was evidently anticipating a difficulty in the way of Onesimus being received, "not now as a servant, but above a servant," etc.

If Philemon would naturally say, I am to receive Onesimus *now*, "not as a servant, but as above a servant," a freed man, a "brother beloved," then he owes me for that time he has been absent. If freedom is claimed for him *now*, I claim compensation for my time;—quite a natural inference. Well, said Paul, "If he oweth thee, I will repay it," witness "mine own hand." "Albeit, I do not say to thee how thou owest unto me thine own self besides." This was a beautiful offsetting of indebtedness. This was jumping the account. Philemon could not have been so stupid as not to see Paul's appreciation of Onesimus' indebtedness to him. This is Paul's verdict in the case. Philemon, your claim upon the person of Onesimus, and my claim upon you, are equal. I do not say that you owe me time-service, or money, but "*thine own self.*" In the light of the gospel, a slaveholders' claim upon the person of his slave, is no better than a preacher's claim upon the person of his convert. If Paul did not intend to make this impression upon Philemon, there is neither sense nor meaning in this part of his epistle to Philemon.

Paul claimed nothing from Philemon but brotherly confidence and affection. And this he required from Philemon toward Onesimus—that he should not now receive him in his former relation of "a servant," but in his new relation, that of a "brother beloved;" and his love to him must be without "dissimulation." This was giving to Onesimus what was "just and equal." This was consenting to the "wholesome words of our Lord Jesus Christ, and the doctrine which was according to godliness." "If any man teach otherwise," etc., "from such withdraw thyself."

If there had been none to advocate slavery in the primitive church, it would have died without a struggle or a groan. For it is not even a presumable case, that under the light of the gospel, and the affection of its early converts, it could have maintained a footing. But it was then as now. There were those who had a large interest in the system. Some were more under the influence of worldly "gain" than the principles of godliness. These would justify this old lucrative practice. Others who had only a collateral interest, or an interest in those who had a direct interest, would put forth the hand of help to "admit and sustain" slavery in the church, as it existed in the State. For in no other sense, and by no other appliances can it exist any where in God's wide universe. To defend its rightful continuance in the church, these teachers were compelled to come in direct conflict with the gospel of Christ; and by false issues, and "wrestings" of the "words of our Lord Jesus Christ," and the "doctrine of godliness," sought to harmonize slavery with christianity. Hence the command to Timothy, and through him to the churches, "*from such withdraw thyself.*"

As I said before, so say I now again, in this teaching we have the *root* of the entire evil, for *the love of slavery is the love of money.*

Let christian principle, in its unchecked, unrestrained power, work, and it will work slavery out of the church now, as it did in the beginning. For we may safely say, there never was a christian slaveholder that had not serious *qualms* of conscience. And if his convictions of what is "*just,*" "*equal,*" and "*godlike,*" were not *blunted* by a false and deceitful philosophy, he would give his guilty conscience ease by the "manumission of all his slaves, as some good men both among the dead and the living have done."

Brethren, there is not in the whole chapter of church discipline, a more clearly defined, and a more important duty, than the prompt withdrawal from every brother who is publicly advocating and teaching the doctrine of human slavery.

And finally, mine answer to such as have asked the question—"How shall we do this?" we say just as you would "withdraw" yourselves from any brother "who is walking disorderly."

And now we ask you, dear brethren, in the name of our insulted christianity, and in behalf of suffering, defrauded, brutalized humanity, *Will you do it?*

APPENDIX.

THE object of the foregoing argument was primarily to defend the Bible—more especially the Old Testament—against the oft-repeated charge of infidel abolitionists, that *the* Book, so called by way of eminence, was the patron of American Slavery. And, as the Bible was the basis of the Church, therefore the Church was the active and efficient bulwark of the system. The careful reader is now prepared to bring in his verdict. If the Bible has been fairly vindicated by the author—as the title of this little volume would modestly assume, then the decision is—*the Bible is not guilty, and this charge of infidels is false.* The testimony may conduct the mind to this conclusion, and yet the charge against the Church may be true in whole, or in part. The Church does assume that the Bible is her basis. But what is assumed, is not always true—only what is proved is true, *always true.* The Church may in the main, rest upon the Bible, but, that all she has taught and practiced, is upon the authority of the Bible is not true. Even the Protestant Church in Protestant America, in days of yore, burned witches, persecuted Quakers and Baptists upon assumed bible authority. The most monstrous things have been said and done under the false pretense of Bible sanction. That the Church should in the year of grace, one thousand eight hundred and fifty-eight, justify slaveholding, would be nothing peculiar in her history. What was true of God's ancient people, may be true of his people now: "All the day long have I stretched out my hand to a disobedient and gainsaying people."

More, infinitely more, is involved in the present controversy, than the rights of masters and the wrongs of slaves. The *credit* of the Bible, the moral standing of the Church, and the *honor* of Jesus Christ are all directly embraced in this issue: 1st. *The credit of the Bible.* If, as many ministers and Church members assume, the teachings of the Scriptures justify slaveholding, then, all opposed to this practice, believing this assumption to be true, must view the Bible with the same abhorrence they do slavery. If there can be such a thing as involuntary infidelity, this must be that thing. No man, surely, could be regarded as being perverse or wicked for condemning the system of human slavery. Nay, opposition to every form of oppression, indicates a good, rather than a wicked heart. It indicates a susceptible conscience—a healthful state of the moral sentiments—therefore, opposition to slavery is a virtue. In this aspect of the subject, a man of a benevolent heart must do violence to the better sentiments of his soul, or he must be an infidel. We are acquainted with some who have become infidels, but not willingly. It was not without a conflict, that they lost confidence in the Bible. But few of the many are capable of critical investigation. Some are wanting in natural discrimination; others have not leisure for laborious investigation. The masses are governed by the few. Whatever may fall into their way, *true* or *false*, upon a controverted question, will place them upon one side or the other, as the case may be.

Suppose such an one should read the volume, entitled "The Philosophy of Slavery as connected with Human Happiness," by James Shannon. The reasoning seems plausible. He is not capable of detecting the sophistry of an artful reasoner. To him, the argument appears sound, and every way conclusive. In despite of his faith, his hope, and his love, he can not escape the conclusion—that the Bible is on the side of slavery. He strives for a time to reconcile this conclusion with his moral sense—his convictions of right. This he can not do, and after long and painful conflict, his baffled, wearied spirit yields to what his own consciousness declares to be right—and "the weak brother perish for whom Christ died." With others who would rather hear what would invalidate the claims of the Bible and justify their wicked lives, the alternatives are easy and soon determined. Hence, it is true that slavery in the Church will insure infidelity in the world.

2d. *The Moral Standing of the Church.* Men of anti-slavery sentiments are greatly embarrassed with the pro-slavery tendency of the Church. When the minister shall class slavery among the sins of the times, some of his church members will cry *nigger* preacher—*nigger* preaching—*political* preaching—agitation, etc., and the balance of the Church have not moral *stamina* to defend the preacher against these assaults. The Churches of the North are in fellowship with the slaveholding Churches of the South. They recognize slaveholders as good and worthy christians. They coöperate with them in Bible and Missionary Societies. And, in fine, slaveholding is not *even* the smallest perceptible *spot* in christian character. Then he looks into the Churches South. Here, he beholds slave-breeding—slave-selling—buying—whipping—hunting, etc. Further, he sees that slave marriages are a *farce*—paternal and filial relations wholly disregarded—education withheld—and every thing managed *just as it is out of the Church.* The effect of this heart-sickening spectacle upon the mind, must be to shock all the moral sensibilities. The conviction must be, that if ever the Church was the the "pillar and support of the truth," *she is not that now.* If such Church members are in a fair way for salvation, I need not be much concerned about my condition. That the Church with all her pro-slavery proclivities, can favorably influence such minds, is not presumable. Here, then, is a large class of the best read and the most intelligent, placed beyond her reach, and will remain out of her pale, until she will remove this "rock of offense," this "stone of stumbling;" and in the ratio of the progress of anti-slavery sentiments, will this class of opponents increase. What a wasting of the Lord's treasures! what a squandering of Church influence! Who will be responsible when the king shall return to reckon with his servants? The Church is required to "walk in wisdom toward them that are without"—to "give no offense to Jew nor Gentile." That mystical body formed by Jesus Christ, of which himself is the head and the heart, presiding over—animating by his good indwelling spirit, should be unblamable and without offense—should be the admiration of all good men—all who can "approve the things that are excellent," "lovely," and of "good report." The Church in her youthful virgin days was *thoroughly anti-slavery*. Her doctrinal standard was the "*wholesome words of our Lord Jesus Christ*," "*and the doctrine which is according to Godliness.*" Those who would not consent to this, but taught a contrary doctrine, were withdrawn from. This is true, in the judgment of *one*, who has *thought* more—*spoken* more—*written* more, and *discriminated* more clearly between the Church in her pure primitive state, and her corrupt modern condition, than any living man. To quote his own language:—"*If any thing is wanting to finish a picture of the most glaring inconsistencies, add to this those christians, who are daily extolling the blessings of civil and religious liberty, and, at the same time, by a system of the most cruel oppression, separating the wife from the embrace of her husband, and the mother from her tender offspring; violating every principle, and rending every tie that endears life and reconciles man to his lot; and that, forsooth, because 'might gives right,' and a man is held guilty because his skin is a shade darker than the standard color of the times. Adverting to these signs of the times, and many others to which these reflections necessarily lead, will you not say, that this prophesy is now fulfilled.*"—2 Tim. iv. 3, 4. "There will be a time when they will not endure wholesome teaching, but having itching ears, they will, according to their own lusts, heap up to themselves teachers. And from the truth, indeed, they will turn away their ears and be turned aside unto fables." "Now from these turn away." *Christian reader, remember this command, and from such turn away.* See "Christian Baptist," eighth edition, page 8.

This is indeed, a most revolting picture. The writer had the *original* before him. Being a citizen of the "Old Dominion" he could look at Church slavery from the right angle of vision. But, in this, as in some other cases, the first view of a revolting scene produces a shock—in the second it is less violent, and by familiarity the first emotions wear away; then for a time we *pity*, then *embrace*. . . . Who is this that violates every principle and rends every tie? They are Christians. Yes, Christians—says the writer. Yes, "Christians who are daily extolling the blessings of civil and religious liberty." Surely, he was not serious when he called those described in the prophecy cited—Christians. If the reader will turn back and read the extract again, he will see that the writer did not regard them as Christians of the olden stamp, but he viewed them in the light of prophecy. On the prophetic chart they stand as apostates,—Christians existing in "perilous times"—times perilous to the souls of believers,—Christians "having a form of godliness, but denying the power thereof,—Christians whose "lustful, itching ears," would not "endure sound teaching," etc.

If the writer of the above extract was correct in the application of Paul's prediction to Timothy, the present slaveholding portion of the Church meets the prophecy. This terrible state of the Church is seen by many of her members. And, because the Church will not "*turn away*" from the thousands who are practising this most "cruel oppression"—"separating husband and wife," they turn away from the Church. And, many sensible persons will not enter, so long as this generally admitted wickedness is continued in

Church fellowship. We justify neither the former nor the latter. But, from this standpoint we can not fail to see and feel the importance of the words of Christ: "Let your light so shine before men, that they may see your good works, and glorify your father which is in heaven."

3d. *The honor of Christ.*—As *the* Book reflects honor or dishonor upon its author, so does the system of morality and religion reflect honor or disgrace upon its originator. If the fanaticism of the Crusaders, the corruptions of the Confessional, and the horrors of the Inquisition, were in harmony with the teachings of Jesus of Nazareth, who, but the most stupid Papist could view him with admiration? If his religion leads to such results, it should be and would be *abjured* by all good men. And, for the same reason all good men must repudiate Christianity, if as some affirm, it sanctions American slavery. If this be true, the Gospel does not, can not commend itself to "every man's conscience in the sight of God." To do this, the Gospel must command what is *right*, both as it respects God and man. Then will it reflect honor upon its author. But, the Gospel of Jesus Christ does *even* more than *this;* it enjoins all that is *pure* and *benignant.* This will be admitted by all men of enlightened reason. But, if Chritianity does permit the opposite, then is *it* a mixed system, and its author a being of a mixed character. It is, we believe, admitted by all, that the religion of Jesus Christ is favorable to civilization. This has been its practical tendency from the beginning. Is it also favorable to *barbarism?* If so, where is the proof? It will also be admitted that the religion of the New Testament promotes both civil and religious liberty. Does it also promote civil and religious bondage? If it promotes both, what a *mighty antagonism* it must be in itself! If so, why are not these warring elements in the system properly classified and arranged? If it embodies such self-contradictory and self-destructive principles, infidels and slaveholding Christians would have brought them to light. If such be the *heterogeneous* character of *the Book*, then, both freedom and slavery are legitimate in Christian practice. Then let the ministers of Jesus Christ so set the instrument as to play the tune that may best suit the times and the occasion.

With this hypothetical *premise* before us, let us look first, at the Christianity of the New Testament; for, that may, or may not be the same as the professed, *ostensible* Christianity of the Church. If it is, what a mass of contradictions; what conflicting, warring elements are contained in this system! Are there to be found in human society, two things more antagonistical than liberty and slavery? Are not these enemies? Can these foes ever be reconciled? Will they ever be brought within an embracing distance? That their anger will never be placated, we need only to look at home. We need not go to distant periods and distant lands. Look into our own States and Churches. What a separating of friends! What a breaking up of friendships! As is the cause, so is the effect, and this effect will continue until the cause is removed, or America shall be suddenly and unexpectedly converted into one *vast Dormitory.* But, so long as society is awake and active, will the strife wax fiercer and fiercer, and the breach become wider and wider. And, inasmuch as our Church religion claims to be the Christian religion, and our *by-law*, or national religion assumes to be the same, Jesus Christ, by fair sequence, is responsible for all these results, if he has incorporated the element of slavery, with that system of morality and piety he has vouchsafed to mankind. If, as is claimed by many who profess to be followers of Christ, they have a divine right from him to be slave masters, then is he so directly involved in the horrors of slavery, that no love for his person, or respect for his authority, as a teacher sent from God, can ever remove this odium from his character.

There is one all-pervading principle in the Bible, but, more fully developed in the teachings of Jesus Christ and his Apostles, that must for ever silence all merely inferential evidence in favor of slavery, drawn from that source. If there were no direct negative testimony, the principle of love to God and man, in the extent and strength of obligation, as enforced in the Gospel, would be an all-sufficient *negation*. If the Gospel claims love from all to all, as will not be denied, then must slaveholding be prompted by love, both upon the part of the master and his slave. This, no sane man will affirm. Therefore, according to the law of Christian love, there can be no such thing as a Christian slaveholder. Christian slaveholder is indeed a contradiction in terms, as truly so as *temperate* drunkard, or *honest* thief.

It may be safely questioned, whether the vaunted benevolence of slaveholders is *even* in the precincts of Christian benevolence. Love must have both a basis and an object. "The world will love its own," said the great Teacher. It will love those of its *clan* or *party*, and then no longer than the love is reciprocal. Is this Christian love? Let Jesus Christ answer. "Love your enemies, bless them that curse you, do good to them that hate you," etc., "that ye may be the children of your Father which is in Heaven." Publicans love Publicans, and Publicans salute Publicans. This is the love of the world. But, Christ said to his Disciples more than this, "Be ye therefore perfect, even as your Father which is in Heaven is perfect." This is the moral of the lesson on love. The premises are, you must love men, "enemies" and all, as God loves them. Your Father in Heaven loves all the just and the unjust; therefore, he is doing them good, makes his "sun to shine upon them," and sends them "rain also." Many of the divine perfections are incommunicable; but his love is transferable. Therefore, the command, "be perfect," is not grievous. Every soul that has enjoyed the full regenerating power of the Gospel, does love all men, friend and enemy, as God loves them; and like Him, will do them good when he can. We might here inquire what is the probable reason of this unlimited love of God to man? Is it simply because he is his creature? God has other creatures besides man. But, for no other being he has made, has he manifested the same degree of love. Perhaps a single sentence will explain this mystery, "And God said, let us make man in our image, after our likeness." . . . This would suggest that God would regard his own image and likeness. That image may have been marred by sin, but the Creator loves it still, and will love it until entirely obliterated. And not only so, he is jealous of his image impressed upon man. He that will damage that likeness shall not go unpunished. "Whoso sheddeth man's blood, by man shall his blood be shed, for in the image of God made he man." "But the tongue can no man tame," etc. "Therewith bless we God even the Father; and therewith curse we men which are made after the similitude of God." The apostle adds immediately, "doth a fountain send forth at the same place sweet water and bitter? The man that will bless God, the Original, and curse man the similitude, is a contradiction in himself. "And every one that loveth him that begat, loveth him also that is begotten of him," for the begotten bears the image of the begetter. He that loves the Creator, must love the creature, made in the similitude of the Creator. He can no more love the one and hate the other, than a fountain can at the same place issue different kinds of water. The love of God and man are therefore inseparable. God has placed the hand and the tongue under an interdict. He has said to these deadly instruments, do mine "image" no harm. In this short inductive argument we have the true reason for God's wondrous love to man, *universal* man, and also the reason for man's love to his fellow man. Can a slaveholder love God? when he chattelizes the image of God in the person of every slave. When he sells a slave he sells God's image. If his conscience will permit him to place the *similitude* upon the auction block and sell it for gold, it would allow him to sell the *Original.* It is not the simple fact of buying or selling humanity that constitutes the offense. It is the object of the sale and purchase that constitutes the real indignity both to God and man. Men have bought wives and servants, for a longer or a shorter period, without insult to the Creator or the creature. The bought and sold continued to be men, were treated and respected as men. But, when a man is sold and bought to be a slave, all human rights and respect cease from that moment and for ever, both as respects himself and his offspring. The similitude of God is quickly converted into the likeness of a beast, to be whipped as beasts, to be held subject to sales private or public, as chattels, goods or things. We must then be permitted to say again, that it may be safely questioned, whether the boasted love of slaveholders makes even an approach to Christian love. And yet more, whether those, who will in any way *aid* or *abet* a system which makes such *havoc* of man, made in the similitude of God, are not greatly wanting in genuine affection for both God and man.

Much that is called love among men is pure selfishness in the sight of God. It is in "word and tongue" *only*, not in heart, not in "deed and truth." All men love some men, but *few* men love and "honor all men," as Jesus Christ has given command and example.

"Thou shalt love the Lord thy God with all thy heart," etc. "Thou shalt love thy neighbor as thyself." "Love worketh no ill to his neighbor." "Who is my neighbor?" "Who was neighbor to him that fell among thieves?" "He that showed mercy on him." "*Go and do thou likewise.*"

DAVENPORT, Jan. 30, 1858. JONAS HARTZEL.

www.ingramcontent.com/pod-product-compliance
Lightning Source LLC
LaVergne TN
LVHW021418110826
845150LV00007B/1987

9781425509361